Carpentry and Joinery

CONSTRUCTION SERIES

Carpentry and Joinery

CONSTRUCTION SERIES

www.skills2learn.com
Experts in e-learning & virtual reality simulation

Australia • Brazil • Japan • Korea • Mexico • Singapore • Spain • United Kingdom • United States

CENGAGE Learning™

Carpentry and Joinery
Skills2Learn

Publishing Director: Linden Harris

Commissioning Editor: Lucy Mills

Development Editor: Helen Green

Editorial Assistant: Claire Napoli

Project Editor: Lucy Arthy

Production Controller: Eyvett Davis

Marketing Manager: Jason Bennett

Typesetter: MPS Limited, a Macmillan Company

Cover design: HCT Creative

Text design: Design Deluxe

© 2012 Cengage Learning EMEA

For product information and technology assistance,
contact **emea.info@cengage.com.**

For permission to use material from this text or product,
and for permission queries,
email **emea.permissions@cengage.com.**

British Library Cataloguing-in-Publication Data

A catalogue record for this book is available from the British Library.

ISBN: 978-1-4080-4187-1

Cengage Learning EMEA

Cheriton House, North Way, Andover, Hampshire, SP10 5BE
United Kingdom

Cengage Learning products are represented in Canada by Nelson Education Ltd.

For your lifelong learning solutions, visit **www.cengage.co.uk**

Purchase your next print book, e-book or e-chapter at **www.cengagebrain.com**

Printed in Malta by Melita Press
1 2 3 4 5 6 7 8 9 10 – 14 13 12

Contents

Foreword

The construction industry is a significant part of the UK economy and a major employer of people. It has a huge impact on the environment and plays a role on our everyday life in some shape or form. With environmental issues such as climate change and sustainable sourcing of materials now playing an important part in the design and construction of buildings and other structures, there is a need to educate and re-educate those new to the industry and those currently involved.

This construction series of e-learning programmes and text workbooks has been developed to provide a structured blended learning approach that will enhance the learning experience and stimulate a deeper understanding of the construction trades and give an awareness of sustainability issues. The content within these learning materials has been aligned to units of the Wood Occupations, National Occupational Standards and can be used as a support tool whilst studying for any relevant vocational qualifications.

The uniqueness of this construction series is that it aims to bridge the gap between classroom-based and practical-based learning. The workbooks provide classroom-based activities that can involve learners in discussions and research tasks as well as providing them with understanding and knowledge of the subject. The e-learning programmes take the subject further, with high quality images, animations and audio further enhancing the content and showing information in a different light. In addition, the e-practical side of the e-learning places the learner in a virtual environment where they can move around freely, interact with objects and use the knowledge and skills they have gained from the workbook and e-learning to complete a set of tasks whilst in the comfort of a safe working environment.

The workbooks and e-learning programmes are designed to help learners continuously improve their skills and provide confidence and a sound knowledge base before getting their hands dirty in the real world.

About the Construction Consortia

This series of construction workbooks and e-learning programmes have been developed by the E-Construction Consortium. The consortium is a group of colleges and organizations that are passionate about the construction industry and are determined to enhance the learning experiences of people within the different trades or those that are new to it.

The consortium members have many years experience in the construction and educational sectors and have created this blended learning approach of interactive e-learning programmes and text workbooks to achieve the aim of:

- Providing accessible training in different areas of construction.
- Bridging the gap between classroom-based and practical-based learning.
- Providing a concentrated set of improvement learning modules.
- Enabling learners to gain new skills and qualifications more effectively.
- Improving functional skills and awareness of sustainability issues within the industry.
- Promoting health and safety in the industry.
- Encouraging training and continuous professional development.

For more information about this construction series please visit: **www.e-construction.co.uk** or **www.skills2learn.com**.

About e-learning

INTRODUCTION

This construction series of workbooks and e-learning programmes uses a blended learning approach to train learners about construction skills. Blended learning allows training to be delivered through different mediums such as books, e-learning (computer-based training), practical workshops, and traditional classroom techniques. These training methods are designed to complement each other and work in tandem to achieve overall learning objectives and outcomes.

E-LEARNING

The Carpentry and Joinery e-learning programme that is also available to sit alongside this workbook offers a different method of learning. With technology playing an increasingly important part of everyday life, e-learning uses visually rich 2D and 3D graphics/animation, audio, video, text and interactive quizzes, to allow you to engage with the content and learn at your own pace and in your own time.

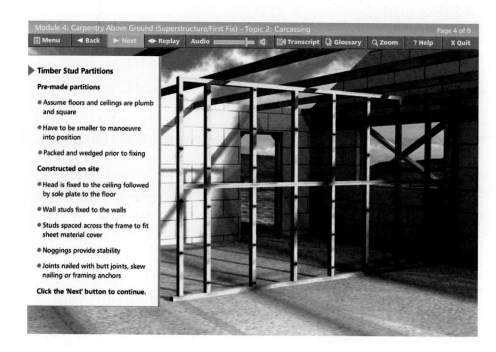

E-PRACTICAL

Part of the e-learning programme is an e-practical interactive scenario. This facility allows you to be immersed in a virtual reality situation where the choices you make affect the outcome. Using 3D technology, you can move freely around the environment, interact with objects, carry out tests, and make decisions and mistakes until you have mastered the subject. By practising in a virtual environment you will not only be able to see what you've learnt but also analyze your approach and thought process to the problem.

BENEFITS OF E-LEARNING

Diversity – E-learning can be used for almost anything. With the correct approach any subject can be brought to life to provide an interactive training experience.

Technology – Advancements in computer technology now allow a wide range of spectacular and engaging e-learning to be delivered to a wider population.

Captivate and Motivate – Hold the learner's attention for longer with the use of high quality graphics, animation, sound and interactivity.

Safe Environment – E-practical scenarios can create environments which simulate potentially harmful real-life situations or replicate a piece of dangerous equipment, therefore allowing the learner to train and gain experience and knowledge in a completely safe environment.

Instant Feedback – Learners can undertake training assessments that feed back results instantly. This can provide information on where they need to re-study or congratulate them on passing the assessment. Results and certificates could also be printed for future records.

On-Demand – Can be accessed 24 hours a day, 7 days a week, 365 days of the year. You can access the content at any time and view it at your own pace.

Portable Solutions – Can be delivered via a CD, website or LMS. Learners no longer need to travel to all lectures, conferences, meetings or training days. This saves many man-hours in reduced travelling, cost of hotels and expenses.

Reduction of Costs – Can be used to teach best practice processes on jobs which use large quantities or expensive materials. Learners can practise their techniques and boost their confidence to a high enough standard before being allowed near real materials.

CARPENTRY AND JOINERY E-LEARNING

The aim of the carpentry and joinery e-learning programme is to enhance a learner's knowledge and understanding of the carpentry trade. The course content is aligned to units from the

Wood Occupations, National Occupational Standards (NOS) so can be used for study towards certification.

The programme gives the learners an understanding of the technicalities of carpentry and joinery as well as looking at sustainability, health and safety and functional skills in an interactive and visually engaging manner. It also provides a 'real-life' scenario where the learner can apply the knowledge gained from the tutorials in a safe yet practical way.

By using and completing this programme, it is expected that learners will:

● Understand the role of the carpenter in the working environment and have knowledge of some of the tools that will be used.

● Be able to explain the choice of materials for a project, calculate the correct quantities, source these from an appropriate supplier and identify the correct disposal method for waste materials.

● Understand the preparation and procedures for substructure and superstructure work.

● Understand the preparation and procedures for finishes and any joinery work.

The e-learning programme is divided into the following learning modules:

● Getting Started
● Tools and Materials
● Carpentry Below Ground (Substructure)
● Carpentry Above Ground (Superstructure / First Fix)
● Finishes (Second Fix)
● End Test
● Interactive E-Practical Scenario

THE CONSTRUCTION SERIES

As part of the construction series the following e-learning programmes and workbooks are available. For more information please contact the sales team on **emea.fesales@cengage.com** or visit the website **www.e-construction.co.uk**.

- Plastering
- Bricklaying
- Carpentry & Joinery
- Painting & Decorating
- Wall & Floor Tiling

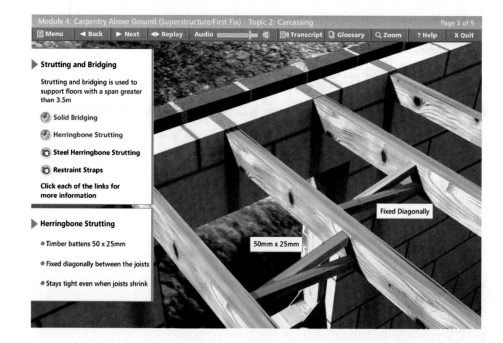

About the NOS

The National Occupational Standards (NOS) provide a framework of information that outline the skills, knowledge and understanding required to carry out work-based activities within a given vocation. Each standard is divided into units that cover specific activities of that occupation. Employers, employees, teachers and learners can use these standards as an information, support and reference resource that will enable them to understand the skills and criteria required for good practice in the workplace.

The standards are used as a basis to develop many vocational qualifications in the United Kingdom for a wide range of occupations. This workbook and associated e-learning programme are aligned to the Wood Occupations, National Occupational Standards, and the information within relates to the following units:

- Conform to General Workplace Safety
- Conform to Efficient Work Practices
- Move and Handle Resources
- Install Frames and Linings
- Install Side Hung Doors
- Install Door Ironmongery
- Install Internal Mouldings
- Install First Fixing Components
- Install Second Fixing Components
- Erect Structural Carcassing Components
- Set Up and Use Circular Saws
- Develop and Maintain Good Working Relationships
- Erect Timber Walls and Floors
- Erect Timber Roof Structures
- Slinging and Signalling the Movement of Loads

About the book

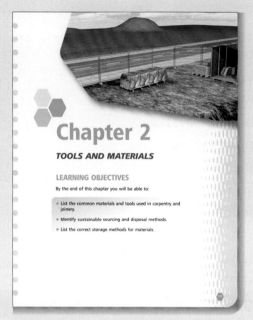

Learning Objectives at the start of each chapter explain the skills and knowledge you need to be proficient in and understand by the end of the chapter.

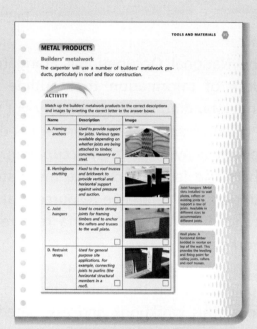

Activities are practical tasks that engage you in the subject and further your understanding.

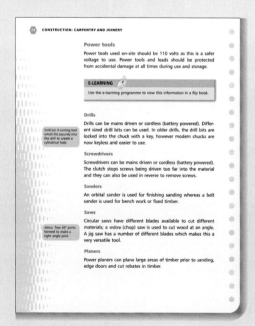

E-Learning Icons link the workbook content to the e-learning programme.

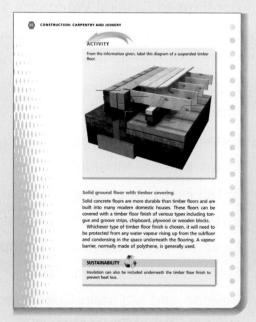

Sustainability Boxes provide information and helpful advice on how to work in a sustainable and environmentally friendly way.

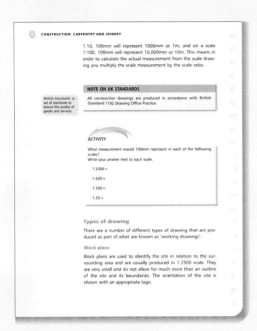

Note on UK Standards draws your attention to relevant building regulations.

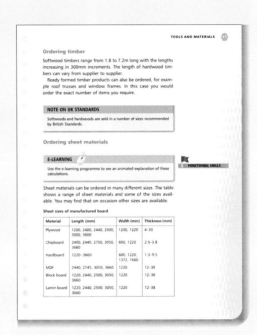

Functional Skills Icons highlight activities that develop and test your Maths, English and ICT key skills.

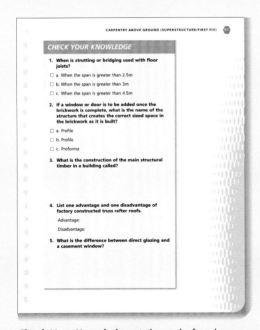

Check Your Knowledge at the end of each chapter to test your knowledge and understanding.

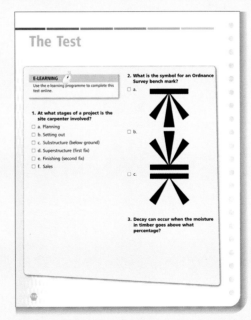

End Test in Chapter 6 checks your knowledge on all the information within the workbook.

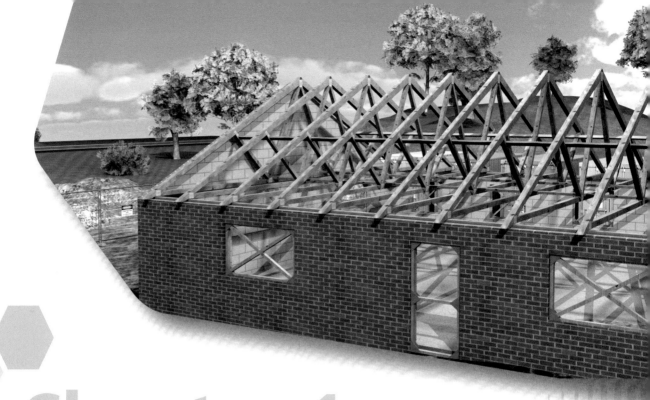

Chapter 1

GETTING STARTED

LEARNING OBJECTIVES

By the end of this chapter you will be able to:

- Explain the role of the carpenter in the construction process.

- Understand the range of processes that the carpenter will be involved in.

- Demonstrate an understanding of the importance of communication with other trades.

NOS REFERENCE

Conform to general workplace safety

Conform to efficient work practices

Develop and maintain good working relationships

INTRODUCTION

The role of the carpenter

Carpentry generally consists of two specialist areas: site carpentry and joinery. Both areas mainly work in wood but can also work with other products, such as metal.

The site carpenter works on a construction site at each stage of the construction process, including setting up the site, first fix and second fix. This can include installing items built off-site by the joiner.

A joiner usually works off-site constructing items like **roof trusses**, window frames, cupboards, staircases and kitchen units.

Roof truss The timber frame structure of a roof, usually factory made and delivered to site.

Skills required by a carpenter

JOB VACANCY

Job Title:
Carpenter
Location:
Nationwide
Hours:
Average 37.5 hours
per week
Work Pattern:
Monday to Friday

Skills Required:
- Fit and healthy
- Practical ability
- Hand-eye
  co-ordination
- Attention to detail
- Numeracy skills
- Part of a team
- Artistic ability
- Working safely

Building design

Each building job will have a design specification document and a bill of quantities which will contain:

- Detailed plans of the build.
- Information on how the construction should be built.
- A list of materials that need to be used and their quantities.

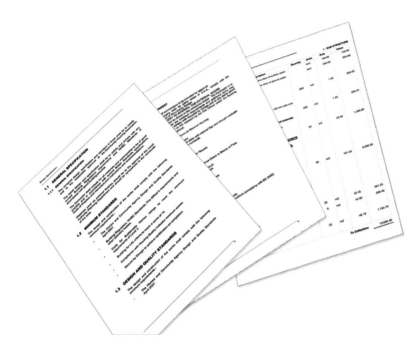

Design specification and bill of quantities

NOTE ON UK STANDARDS

These documents will be required to satisfy and comply with building regulations and meet the approval of local authorities. You will need to refer to and understand these documents to make sure the building is constructed correctly.

Scale drawings

FUNCTIONAL SKILLS

It would be impractical to produce building drawings to their full size so they are reduced to a ratio of the real size, known as a scale drawing. For example, in a drawing to a scale of

1:10, 100mm will represent 1000mm or 1m, and on a scale 1:100, 100mm will represent 10,000mm or 10m. This means in order to calculate the actual measurement from the scale drawing you multiply the scale measurement by the scale ratio.

British Standards A set of standards to ensure the quality of goods and services.

NOTE ON UK STANDARDS

All construction drawings are produced in accordance with **British Standard** 1192 Drawing Office Practice.

ACTIVITY

What measurement would 100mm represent in each of the following scales?
Write your answer next to each scale.

1:2500 =

1:500 =

1:200 =

1:20 =

Types of drawing

There are a number of different types of drawing that are produced as part of what are known as 'working drawings'.

Block plans

Block plans are used to identify the site in relation to the surrounding area and are usually produced in 1:2500 scale. They are very small and do not allow for much more than an outline of the site and its boundaries. The orientation of the site is shown with an appropriate logo.

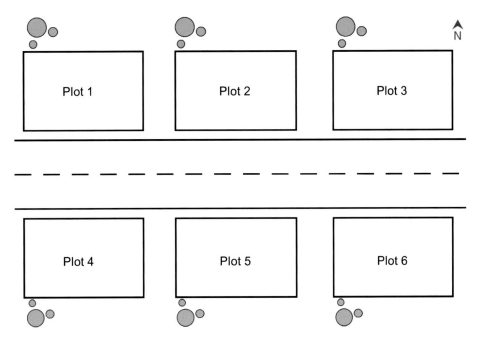

Example of a block plan

Site plans

Site plans show the position of the proposed building on the site as well as proposed roads, drainage and service layouts. They are usually produced in 1:500 scale and again the orientation should be included.

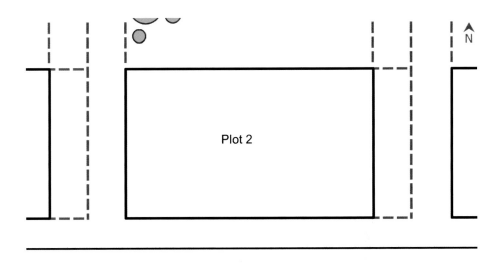

Example of a site plan

Plan drawings

Plan drawings show a bird's-eye view of a building including all rooms, windows and doors. They are produced in 1:200 scale and usually match the elevation drawings.

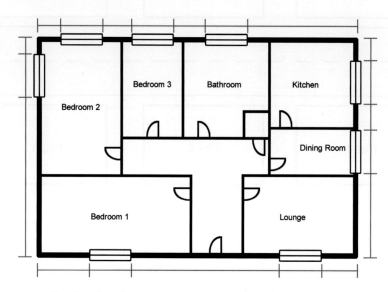

Example of a plan drawing

Elevation drawings

Elevation drawings show the exterior of a building from all sides and include all measurements.

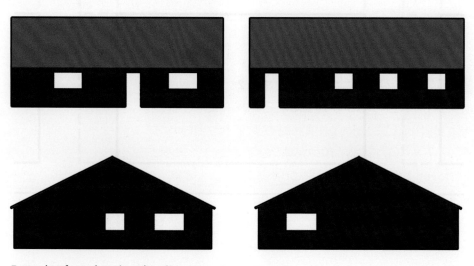

Example of an elevation drawing

Cross section drawings

Cross section drawings show details that would not show on plan and elevation drawings. A scale is chosen to show information that could not be included in other drawings.

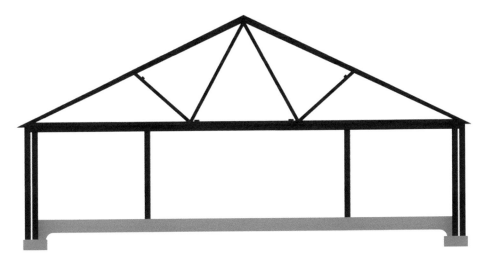

Example of a cross section drawing

Assembly drawings

Assembly drawings show the detailed information at the junction between different elements and components of a building. These are very important drawings and show exactly how the architect wants the building to be constructed and what materials should be used. They are produced in 1:20 scale.

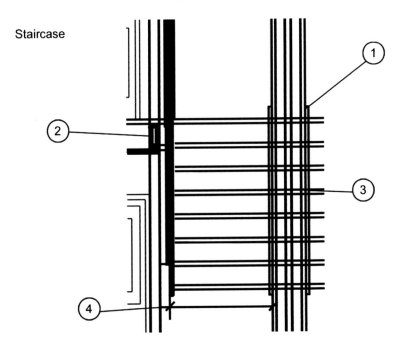

Example of an assembly drawing

ACTIVITY

What does your home look like? Try drawing plan and elevation diagrams of your house.

SETTING UP THE SITE

Temporary structures

The carpenter is usually the first on-site and the last to leave. Before any construction work can begin, the carpenter may need to install some temporary structures including the site offices, washing and toilet facilities for the construction workers and hoardings. The carpenter may also be required to build temporary protective storage areas for materials.

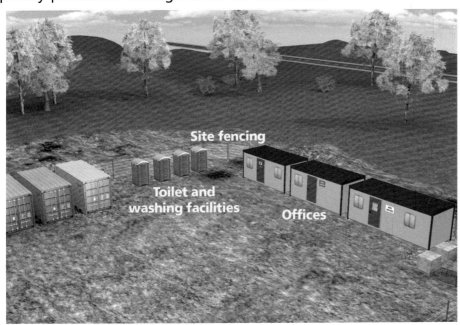

Temporary on-site structures

On-site notices and warnings

HEALTH & SAFETY

An electricity supply will be provided from the main grid. Where this supply reaches the site, the site carpenter will need to build a secure temporary housing for it. The carpenter may also be asked to erect health and safety notice boards across the site.

Temporary electrical supply

Ordnance Survey Bench Marks (OSBMs) Measure height of the land above or below mean sea level.

Ordnance Datum Newlyn The national height system for Great Britain which takes its base height from Newlyn in Cornwall.

Ordnance Datum Newlyn

Ordnance Survey Bench Marks or OSBMs are part of the **Ordnance Datum Newlyn** and record height above or below the average sea level in Newlyn, Cornwall.

Newlyn, Cornwall

Where UK mean sea level is measured

OSBM symbol

NOTE ON UK STANDARDS

It is essential that levels are established before construction begins, and then throughout the process to completion of the building, to ensure the building is level and that there is the correct fall for drainage into existing services. This is achieved using the datum points or bench-marks which have been mapped across the UK by Ordnance Survey.

Level The horizontal level of a surface or structure.

WEBLINKS

More information can be found at the Ordnance Survey website.

www.ordnancesurvey.co.uk

Ordnance Survey Bench Marks

Ordnance Survey Bench Marks are generally cut into churches, public buildings or sometimes concrete pedestals. The height of a bench mark can then be established from an ordnance survey map or by contacting the local authority planning office.

Fundamental Bench Marks (FBMs) These bench marks are the realization of Ordnance Datum Newlyn across the country, from which many thousands of lower order bench marks have been created.

There are around 190 **Fundamental Bench Marks** or FBMs across the country which are maintained to ensure high accuracy.

Tens of thousands of lower order bench marks have been created from the FBMs but there has been little maintenance on these for over 30 years. Property development and road widening has moved and destroyed many of these lower order benchmarks and they should not be relied on for accuracy.

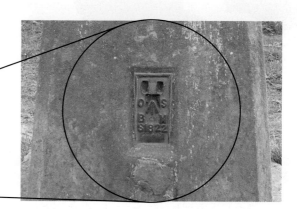

OSBM symbol cut into a pedestal

ACTIVITY

How would you locate your nearest Fundamental Bench Mark? Write your answer below.

Site datum

A reference point or site datum is created on-site before construction begins and usually marks a convenient height, e.g. the finished floor level. The height is calculated from the nearest Ordnance Survey Bench Mark and is represented on-site by a wooden peg set in concrete. The temporary datum peg must be positioned where it will not be disturbed by any construction activity and should be protected by a small wooden fence.

Datum peg Square timber peg used to mark the height of the brickwork up to damp proof course (DPC) level.

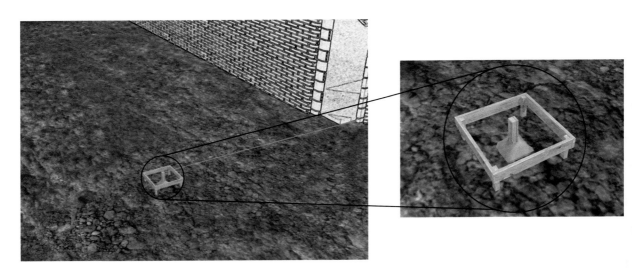

Site datum peg

COMMUNICATION

Communication with other trades

The site carpenter is on-site throughout the construction process. This makes it essential that communication with the other on-site trades is clear and timely. Poor communication can lead to work being delayed or stopped completely and mistakes can be made, which then puts pressure on the budget and timescale of the project.

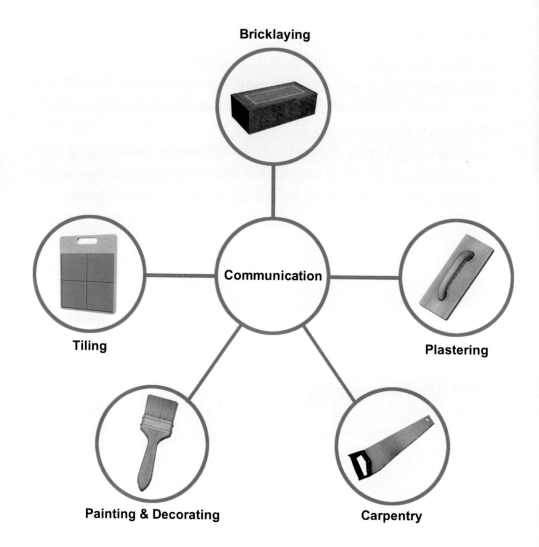

Communicating with other people

It is also important that the correct form of communication is used for the situation. For example, where a record of the communication is needed, a written form of communication should be used. For more sensitive communication where tone of voice or body language may be important, a verbal communication method may be better. Good planning, preparation and communication of tasks on-site will allow work to be carried out efficiently.

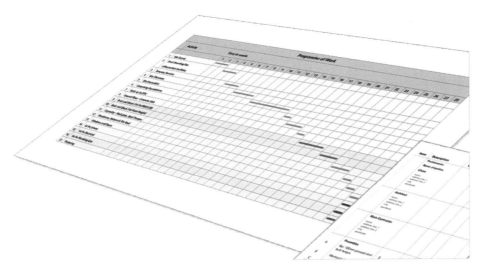

Example of work documents

ACTIVITY

List the different types of communication you would use at work and the situations in which you would use them.

CHECK YOUR KNOWLEDGE

1. Where can you find out the height of an Ordnance Survey Bench Mark?

☐ a. On the concrete pedestal

☐ b. Local authority planning office

☐ c. Ordnance survey map

2. Which of these are forms of written communication?

☐ a. Email

☐ b. Letter

☐ c. Meeting

☐ d. Phone call

☐ e. Radio/Walkie talkie

☐ f. Site plan

☐ g. Work schedule

3. If 100mm on a drawing represents 10m on-site, which scale is being used?

1: _____

4. A bill of quantities will contain a list of _____ that need to be used and their _____

5. Where should the temporary datum peg be positioned?

Chapter 2

TOOLS AND MATERIALS

LEARNING OBJECTIVES

By the end of this chapter you will be able to:

- List the common materials and tools used in carpentry and joinery.

- Identify sustainable sourcing and disposal methods.

- List the correct storage methods for materials.

Sustainable materials Materials that have been sourced by causing little or no damage to the environment.

Ironmongery Products that have been manufactured from metal.

NOS REFERENCE

Conform to general workplace safety

Set up and use circular saws

Move and handle resources

Install door **ironmongery**

TOOLS

The carpenter will use a range of hand and power tools in the course of his work. Each will have its own health and safety considerations.

HEALTH & SAFETY

- Are you familiar with the tool?
- Have you had the appropriate training?
- Is the tool working correctly?
- Is the tool connected to a safe power supply?
- Do you have the correct PPE?
- Do you know the procedure in the event of an accident?

A selection of PPE

Hand tools

The carpenter will use a large number of hand tools during the course of his work.

Saws

Hand saws include cross cut saws which are used to cut across the grain, and rip saws which are used to cut along the grain.

Tenon saws are used to cut tenons and small pieces of wood, whereas dovetail saws are used for small accurate work and dovetails. Coping saws are used to cut curved shapes in wood.

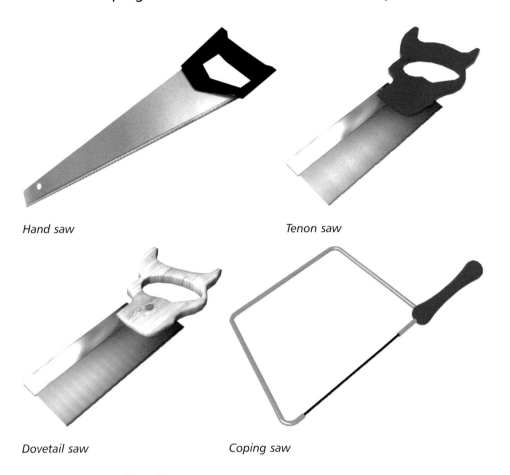

Hand saw

Tenon saw

Dovetail saw

Coping saw

Hammers and mallets

The claw hammer is the most commonly used hammer in joinery and carpentry and is available in different sizes. A pin hammer is used for panel pins, wooden mallets are used in conjunction with chisels whereas rubber mallets are used for tapping joints into place.

Pin hammer

Claw hammer

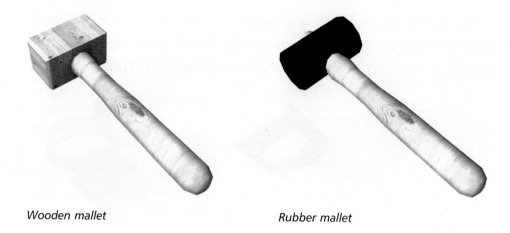

Wooden mallet

Rubber mallet

Planes

A jack plane is used to remove excess wood and flatten sawn timber whereas a smoothing plane is used on wood which has already been planed to give a quality finish. A block plane is used on the ends of timber and for small jobs.

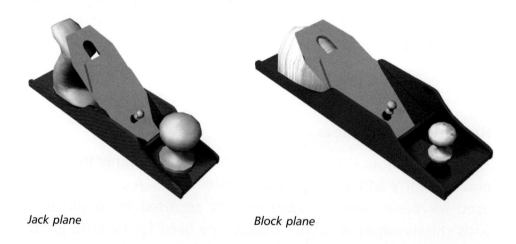

Jack plane

Block plane

Chisels

A bevel edged chisel is used for acute corners and paring. A firmer chisel is used for general bench and site work and is stronger than a bevel edged chisel. A mortise chisel is used to cut out mortise joints and slots.

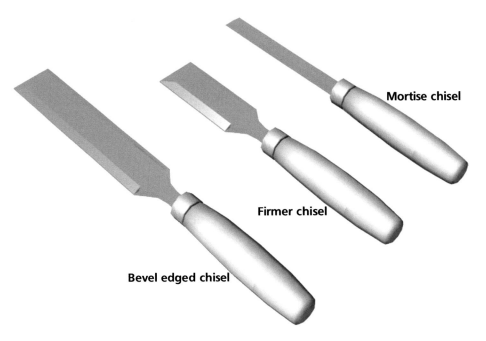

Mortise chisel

Firmer chisel

Bevel edged chisel

A selection of chisels

Boring tools

A wheel brace is used with HSS (high speed steel) drill bits to drill holes up to 10mm. A swing brace can be used with an auger bit for larger holes.

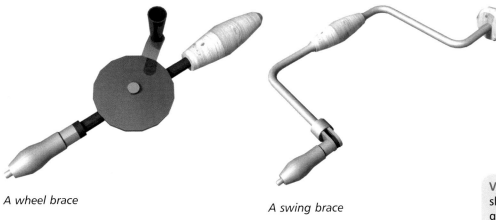

A wheel brace

A swing brace

Veneer Very thin sheets of finely grained woods used to improve the aesthetics and strength of sheet materials, e.g. blockboard.

Measuring and gauging tools

Retractable tape measures and steel rules are used for measuring. Try and combination squares are used to measure 90° and 45° angles. Gauges are used to mark wood and veneers, spirit levels are used to check horizontal levels and plumb items are used to check vertical lines.

Spirit level A tool used to check true vertical and horizontal lines indicated by a bubble in spirit-filled vials.

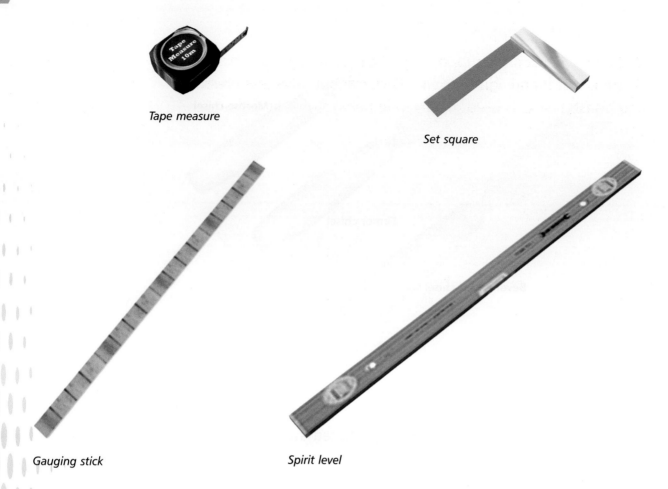

Tape measure

Set square

Gauging stick

Spirit level

Screwdrivers

The carpenter will use a range of screwdrivers. The length of the screwdriver and the head type will depend on the screw being used and the material it is being screwed into.

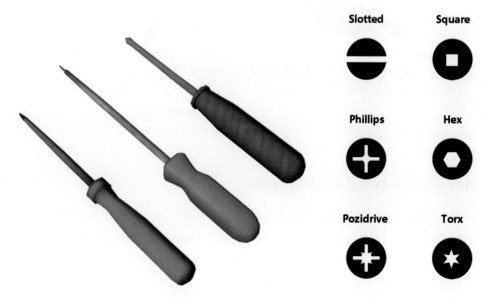

Selection of screwdrives and types of screw heads

Clamps and holding tools

G-clamps are used for supporting small carpentry work. A speed clamp is faster and lighter than a G-clamp but gives less pressure and a sash clamp is used mainly in joinery to hold larger carpentry work.

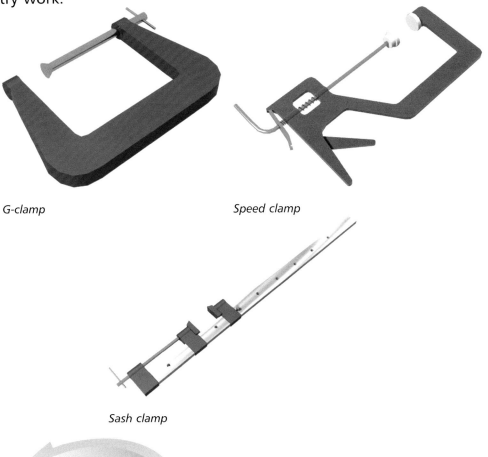

G-clamp

Speed clamp

Sash clamp

ACTIVITY

List the hand tools that are new to you and then use an internet search engine to find out where they would be used and the health and safety considerations for each.

Power tools

Power tools used on-site should be 110 volts as this is a safer voltage to use. Power tools and leads should be protected from accidental damage at all times during use and storage.

E-LEARNING

Use the e-learning programme to view this information in a flip book.

Drills

Drills can be mains driven or cordless (battery powered). Different sized **drill bits** can be used. In older drills, the drill bits are locked into the chuck with a key, however modern chucks are now keyless and easier to use.

> **Drill bit** A cutting tool which fits securely into the drill to create a cylindrical hole.

Screwdrivers

Screwdrivers can be mains driven or cordless (battery powered). The clutch stops screws being driven too far into the material and they can also be used in reverse to remove screws.

Sanders

An orbital sander is used for finishing sanding whereas a belt sander is used for bench work or fixed timber.

Saws

Circular saws have different blades available to cut different materials; a **mitre** (chop) saw is used to cut wood at an angle. A jig saw has a number of different blades which makes this a very versatile tool.

> **Mitre** Two 45° joints formed to make a right angle joint.

Planers

Power planers can plane large areas of timber prior to sanding, edge doors and cut rebates in timber.

Routers

Routers have many different accessories for a wide range of uses including cutting mouldings, recesses and edge trimming.

A collection of power tools

ACTIVITY

List the power tools that are new to you and then use an internet search engine to find out where they would be used and the health and safety considerations for each.

WEBLINKS

TIMBERS

Classification of timber

Timber falls into two main categories: softwood and hardwood. Softwood comes from evergreen (**coniferous**) conifer-type trees such as pine, spruce and larch. It has a simple structure, is easy to work with, grows quickly and is less expensive than hardwood which makes it in high demand for construction work such as roof trusses, staircases and floor **joists**.

Coniferous tree A type of evergreen tree which produces its fruit in the form of cones.

Joist A beam that supports a ceiling or floor.

A type of softwood, Douglas fir

Deciduous trees
Trees which lose all of their leaves for part of the year.

Hardwood comes from broad leafed **deciduous trees** such as oak, beech and mahogany. It has a more complex structure, can be more difficult to work with and due to cost and sustainability is more often used for high quality joinery work like cabinet making.

A type of hardwood, Ash

ACTIVITY

List all the different types of hardwoods and softwoods you can think of in the table. Use a search engine to see if you can find any other types that you don't know of.

Hardwoods	Softwoods

WEBLINKS

Moisture in timber

The moisture content of timber is expressed as a percentage of the dry weight of the timber.

$$\% = (wet\ weight - dry\ weight \times 100)/dry\ weight$$

Timber is dried or seasoned in a number of ways including air or **natural seasoning** and **kiln seasoning**. However, both methods can be used in conjunction with each other.

FUNCTIONAL SKILLS

Air (natural) seasoning The means of drying timber by exposing it to the air and storing in a clean and dry place.

Kiln seasoning The means of drying timber by exposing it to heat using a number of techniques.

Natural 'air' seasoning

Kiln seasoning is more popular in a commercial environment as there is more control over the process. In either case, the end result of the seasoning process should be to arrive at a moisture content of below 20 per cent to prevent decay of the timber, but high enough that the timber will not absorb moisture from its surroundings once it is in place. This is known as having the moisture content 'in equilibrium'.

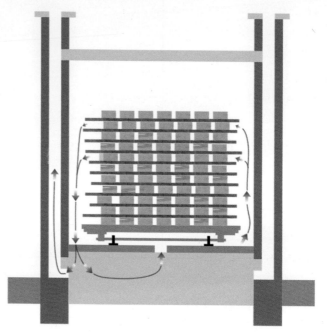

Kiln seasoning

ACTIVITY

What is the moisture content of a timber sample with a wet weight of 26g and a dry weight of 20g?
  Show your working out below.

Is this moisture content low enough to prevent decay?
Write your answer below.

Decay of timber

The decay of timber is usually caused by wood boring insects or a wood rotting fungus. There are a number of insects that destroy wood. Beetles are a common problem and they attack the wood by laying larvae into cracks and splits, the larvae then hatch and bore holes and tunnels into the wood. The ways to prevent this are to try and keep the moisture content of the wood below 10 per cent or by treating the wood with preservative.

Fungal decay, typically wet or dry rot, occurs where conditions are wet or when the moisture content of wood has increased to more than 20 per cent and there is poor ventilation, e.g. a poorly ventilated, humid environment like a bathroom or a persistently leaking drainpipe which allows water to run onto a window frame.

Wet rot is not as serious as dry rot but both conditions should be treated by eliminating the source of moisture through increased ventilation and repair of any leaks, removing the affected timber, cleaning and treating the affected and surrounding area, treating the remaining timber with an appropriate **fungicide** and replacing the damaged timber with new treated timber.

Fungicide A chemical used to kill or slow down fungal decay on timber.

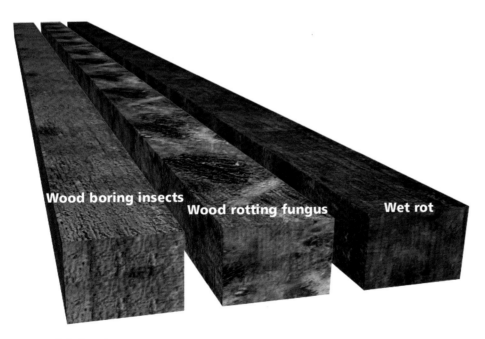

Types of timber decay

WEBLINKS

ACTIVITY

Use an internet search engine to research some appropriate fungicides used to treat wet rot and dry rot.

List your findings below.

SHEET MATERIALS

Types of sheet material

All sheet materials are constructed using glue and the type of glue used will determine whether the sheet material is to be used inside or outside a building. Weather or moisture resistant sheets are constructed using waterproof glue while interior grades of sheets are constructed using normal grade glue. Most modern boards are available in a variety of different surface finishes including colour, type of wood and an applied topcoat, e.g. white faced laminate.

HEALTH & SAFETY

Wearing suitable **PPE** is advisable when working with sheet materials, in particular MDF when a dust mask is essential. The carpenter should use correct manual handling techniques when lifting any materials and should not lift anything heavier than 25kg without help.

PPE The standard and widely used abbreviation for Personal Protective Equipment.

Plywood

Plywood is constructed from thin sheets or veneers glued together, with each sheet at right angles to the previous one to give equal strength across the board. There is usually a minimum of three layers and generally an odd number of layers so that the grain of the outside layers runs in the same direction.

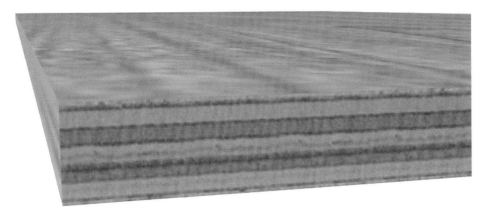

Plywood sheet material

Block board

Block board has a core of a glued layer of wooden strips 19–30mm wide enclosed within a facing veneer of single or double ply. The grain of the veneer runs at right angles to the grain of the wooden strips.

Block board sheet material

Lamin board

Lamin board is constructed in the same way as block board but the core wooden strips do not exceed 7mm in width.

Lamin board sheet material

Chipboard

Chipboard is made from wood chips from softwoods which are combined with a synthetic resin glue and compressed under great pressure and heat to form a board. The board is then sanded and cut to size. Waterproof chipboard is used in humid or damp conditions.

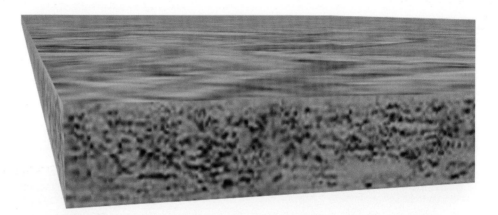

Chipboard

Hardboard

Hardboard is a type of fibreboard produced by a wet process. The wood is shredded into fibres and then pressed using the natural properties of the wood to bind the fibres together into a board. Hardboard is produced in five grades for different purposes.

Hardboard

MDF (Medium Density Fibreboard)

MDF is a fibreboard produced by a dry process where the wood fibres are bound together using a synthetic **adhesive**. MDF has a wide range of uses. However, the dust created when machining MDF is **carcinogenic** and therefore the use of it is listed as a health risk so the correct PPE is essential.

Adhesive General term for a range of bonding agents.

Carcinogenic Chemicals or materials which can increase the risk of cancer. Personal protective equipment should always be worn whenever working with chemicals or materials that are carcinogenic.

MDF (Medium Density Fibreboard)

Cement board

Cement board is made from a combination of **cement** and glass fibres formed into sheets. It is typically used as a tile backing board in kitchens and bathrooms.

Cement A grey or white powdery material made from chalk or limestone and clay. Cement is the most common binder in bricklaying mortar and works by hardening as a result of a chemical reaction when mixed with water. The most common type of cement is Ordinary Portland Cement (OPC).

Cement board

Stirling board

Stirling board is a wood-based board made from softwood strands compressed and bonded together with exterior grade, water resistant resin. It is generally used in areas where appearance is not a priority.

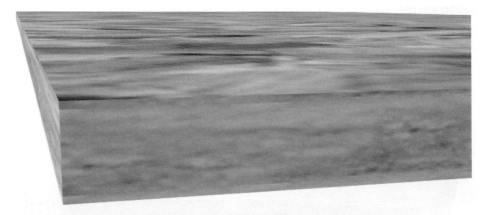

Stirling board

ACTIVITY

WEBLINKS

Use an internet search engine to find out more information about each type of board, list their advantages and disadvantages and where they can be used.

METAL PRODUCTS

Builders' metalwork

The carpenter will use a number of builders' metalwork products, particularly in roof and floor construction.

ACTIVITY

Match up the builders' metalwork products to the correct descriptions and images by inserting the correct letter in the answer boxes.

Name	Description	Image
A. *Framing anchors*	*Used to provide support for joists. Various types available depending on whether joists are being attached to timber, concrete, masonry or steel.* ☐	☐
B. *Herringbone strutting*	*Fixed to the roof trusses and brickwork to provide vertical and horizontal support against wind pressure and suction.* ☐	☐
C. *Joist hangers*	*Used to create strong joints for framing timbers and to anchor the rafters and trusses to the wall plate.* ☐	☐
D. Restraint straps	*Used for general purpose site applications. For example, connecting joists to purlins (the horizontal structural members in a roof).* ☐	☐

Joist hangers Metal slots installed to wall plates, rafters or existing joists to support a row of joists. Available in different sizes to accommodate different joists.

Wall plate A horizontal timber bedded in mortar on top of the wall. This provides the levelling and fixing point for ceiling joists, rafters and roof trusses.

Lintel A horizontal beam of timber (old buildings), stone, concrete or steel (new buildings) spanning the openings, e.g. doors and windows in a wall to support the structure above.

Name	Description	Image
E. *Lintels*	*Used to create simple structural joints and enable simple structures to be created on-site.*	
F. *Angle plates*	*Provide support for an opening in masonry.*	
G. Nail plates	*Prevents sideways movement or buckling in joists over 3m in length.*	

Ironmongery

All ironmongery is available in a wide variety of materials and finishes from plastic to gold plated; the quality of ironmongery chosen will usually be decided by the location where it is to be used.

E-LEARNING

Use the e-learning programme to view this information in a flip book.

Hinges

Hinges are used to fix the door to the frame and to allow the door to open and close. There are various types including steel butt hinges, rising butt hinges, falling butt hinges and strap hinges.

Steel butt hinge

Rising steel butt hinge

Falling steel butt hinge

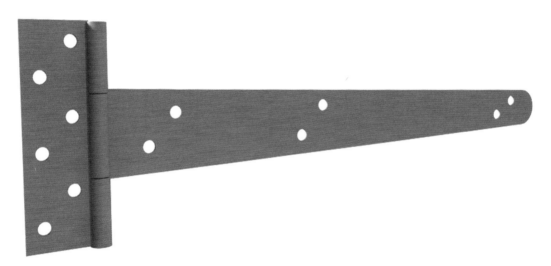

Strap hinge

Locks and latches

Locks and latches are used to fasten doors closed. There are various types available including mortice dead locks, mortice lock latches, mortice latches, night cylinder locks and sliding door locks. Each provides a different level of security depending on the location, e.g. a garden shed or high security storage facility.

Mortice dead lock

Mortice lock latch

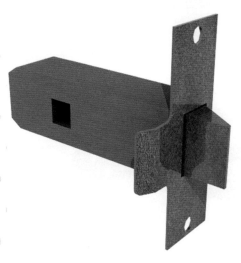

Mortice latch

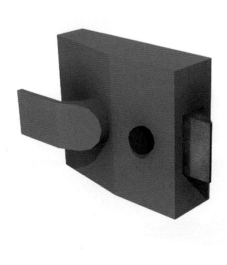

Night cylinder locks

Sliding door lock

Bolts and hooks

Bolts and hooks are two other methods of fastening doors. There are various types available including indicator bolts, barrel bolts, hinge bolts, cabin hooks and suffolk latches.

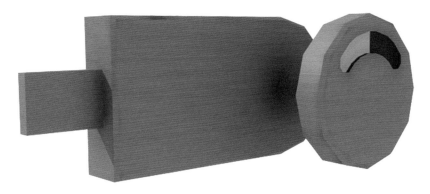

Indicator bolt

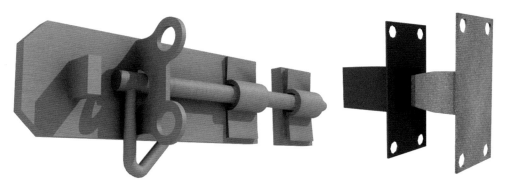

Barrel bolt

Hinge bolt

Cabin hook

Suffolk latch

Door furniture

Door furniture has a number of different uses and includes door knobs and levers, for-end sets, pull handles, letter plates and escutcheon plates. As these items are designed to be decorative and visible the quality is of higher importance than with some other ironmongery products.

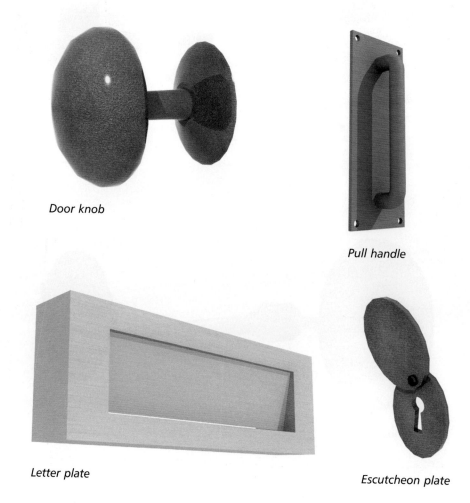

Door knob

Pull handle

Letter plate

Escutcheon plate

Springs and closers

Springs and closers are used to either close doors automatically or hold them open. They include door springs, door closers, door selectors and holder backs which are often used as fire prevention methods.

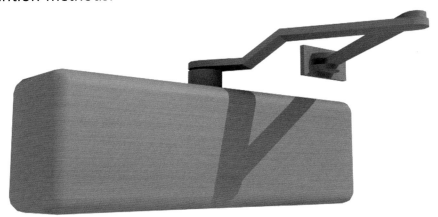

Door closer

ACTIVITY

Can you think of any other forms of ironmongery and where they might be used? Write your ideas below.

ORDERING OF MATERIALS

Sustainable sourcing

SUSTAINABILITY

Approximately 1.6 billion cubic metres of timber is harvested annually worldwide and approximately 50 million cubic metres of this will be

FSC Forest Stewardship Council.

used in the UK. While there is some debate on the sources of wood, there are still reports of timber entering the UK that has been illegally logged. The Forest Stewardship Council or **FSC** is a non-governmental organization that is working to combat illegal, unethical and environmentally damaging logging. When buying new timber, you should look out for the FSC mark to guarantee the source of the timber.

WEBLINKS

Visit the Forest Stewardship Council website to find out more information.

www.fsc-uk.org

ACTIVITY

Where do you think most of the world's timber comes from? Mark on the map the areas that you think supply the world's timber.

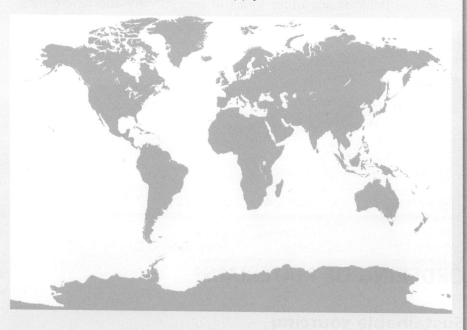

Ordering timber

Softwood timbers range from 1.8 to 7.2m long with the lengths increasing in 300mm increments. The length of hardwood timbers can vary from supplier to supplier.

Ready formed timber products can also be ordered, for example roof trusses and window frames. In this case you would order the exact number of items you require.

NOTE ON UK STANDARDS

Softwoods and hardwoods are sold in a number of sizes recommended by British Standards.

Ordering sheet materials

E-LEARNING

Use the e-learning programme to see an animated explanation of these calculations.

FUNCTIONAL SKILLS

Sheet materials can be ordered in many different sizes. The table shows a range of sheet materials and some of the sizes available. You may find that on occasion other sizes are available.

Sheet sizes of manufactured board

Material	Length (mm)	Width (mm)	Thickness (mm)
Plywood	1200, 2400, 2440, 2500, 3000, 3600	1200, 1220	4–30
Chipboard	2400, 2440, 2750, 3050, 3660	600, 1220	2.5–3.8
Hardboard	1220–3660	600, 1220, 1372, 1660	1.3–9.5
MDF	2440, 2745, 3050, 3660	1220	12–38
Block board	1220, 2440, 2500, 3050, 3660	1220	12–38
Lamin board	1220, 2440, 2500, 3050, 3660	1220	12–38

To calculate the sheet material required to cover an area you need to divide the area to be covered by the area of one sheet.

Sheet materials required = Area to cover/Area of one sheet

Taking a common size for sheet materials 2440mm × 1220mm– the area of the sheet is 2.97m²	2440 × 1220 = 2976800mm² or 2.97m²
To cover a floor area of 96m² divide 96 by 2.97 which gives us 32.3, which we round up to 33 to give us a whole number. Therefore we need to order 33 sheets of material.	96m²/2.97m² = 32.3, rounded up to 33

The waste is calculated by subtracting the area of sheet material used from the total area of the sheets ordered.

Waste = Area ordered − Area used

In the example above the order is for 33 sheets of material which are 2.97m² giving a total area of 98.01m²	33 × 2.97m² = 98.01m²
Therefore using 98.01m² to cover the floor leaves wastage of 2.01m²	98.01m² − 96m² = 2.01m²

ACTIVITY

Using 2440mm × 1220mm sheets, how many sheets would you need to order to cover an area of 150m²?
Show your working out below.

Ordering ironmongery

Ironmongery is ordered according to the door schedule of a project. This is a table that lists all the doors that are to be fitted into a building using the numbers D1, D2, D3 up to the total number of doors. The type of ironmongery needed for each door will be listed, sometimes with brand names and part numbers. By listing the ironmongery needed for each door you can order the exact number of each component needed and there should be no wastage.

Example door schedule

Description	D1	D2	D3	D4	D5
Steel butt hinges		×3	×3	×3	×3
Mortice dead lock	×1				
Letter plate	×1				
Indicator bolt			×1		

ACTIVITY

Using the door schedule table shown above, research prices online or in a catalogue and then complete the following order form, making sure you note down where you find each price.

MATERIALS ORDER FORM			
Order No: Date:			
Site Address:			
Site Name/Address of Supplier:			
Please supply the following order to the above address:			
Description:	**Quantity:**	**Cost per item (£):**	**Total:**
Total Cost:			
VAT:			
Final Cost inc VAT:			

STORAGE OF MATERIALS

Storage of timbers

E-LEARNING

Use the e-learning programme to see an animated explanation of storage of timbers.

Timbers should be stored outside in a secure location on timber bearers that are clear of the ground. The ground should be vegetation free and this can be helped by adding a layer of gravel on the ground before stacking the timbers.

The timbers should be stacked with piling sticks between each layer to provide support and to allow air to circulate. Finally, the stack should be under a covered framework to protect it from the weather but arranged to still allow a flow of air to prevent condensation forming. Timely ordering of timbers avoids prolonged storage times.

Storage of timber

Storage of sheet materials

E-LEARNING

Use the e-learning programme to see an animated explanation of storage of sheet materials.

Sheet materials should be stored in a dry, well ventilated environment. They should be stacked on timber cross bearers which are the right distance apart for the material being stored to prevent sagging. They should also be separated by sticks at regular intervals to allow the circulation of air but these must be in line with the bearers to prevent distortion of the sheets.

If space is short sheet materials can be stored upright in specially made racks, which must be the correct size to prevent bowing of the materials while still allowing easy access and removal. Sheet materials with a finished surface should be stored face to face to prevent damage and different types of sheet material should be separated.

Sheet material stored in stacks

Sheet material stored in racks

DISPOSAL OF MATERIALS

Landfill

SUSTAINABILITY

The UK construction industry produces over 36 million tonnes of landfill waste every year. Sources of waste vary depending on the phase of construction, the method and the type of building, but most waste is produced through over ordering, damage by mishandling, inadequate storage or weather damage.

Unnecessary packaging of construction materials also contributes a large amount of waste. For companies that meet the criteria, the law in the form of the **packaging directive** controls the amount of timber from pallets and packing crates that can be disposed of in landfill or incinerated. The directive sets recycling and recovery targets for the amount of wood used in packaging in the UK and the latest targets can be found online.

Packaging directive
A government enforced directive which aims to control the amount of packaging which can be disposed of in landfill.

ACTIVITY

Use an internet search engine to find the latest targets for the packaging directive and make a note of the URL below.

Waste minimization strategies

SUSTAINABILITY

There are three basic ways of dealing with waste: Reduce, Reuse, Recycle.

The prevention of waste in the first place is the ideal solution; this can be achieved by identifying possible waste streams early on in the build process. It is estimated that over ordering leads to 13 million tonnes of new building materials being wasted every year. Improved communication between everyone involved in a build can ensure exact calculations of required materials are made and that unnecessary waste is prevented. Carefully timed deliveries can help to reduce waste caused by inadequate storage and damage.

In the case of timber, the source should also be checked to ensure it is sustainable and in renovation projects reclaimed timber products can be sourced from architectural salvage companies.

Once waste has been created, one solution to managing it is to reuse it. Many materials can be reclaimed and possibly sold to offset the costs of a building project. For example, in renovation projects, floor boards, window and door frames, doors and staircases can be sold to architectural salvage companies.

Recycling is another option for managing waste. Materials that can be recycled need to be identified early on the build process and separated from the other materials for easy storage, collection and transfer. An effective recycling strategy needs links to established local recycling facilities and contractors. Use of recycled materials on-site can reduce cost and wood that is of sufficient quality can be sold as reclaimed timber. Where the wood is of insufficient quality it can be recycled as mulch, a composting agent, pet bedding, equestrian surfacing, chipboard or MDF.

ACTIVITY

Locate your nearest architectural salvage company or timber recycling company and find out what they do and how they make use of left over materials. Make some notes here.

CHECK YOUR KNOWLEDGE

1. **The use of which sheet material is listed as a health risk?**

    ☐ a. Block board

    ☐ b. Cement board

    ☐ c. Chipboard

    ☐ d. Hardboard

    ☐ e. Lamin board

    ☐ f. MDF

    ☐ g. Stirling board

    ☐ h. Plywood

2. **How many whole 2.97m² sheets of material would you need to cover a floor area of 150m²?**

3. **Sheet materials can be stored vertically as well as horizontally.**

   ☐ a. True

   ☐ b. False

4. **List three possible uses for wood that is of insufficient quality to be recycled as timber.**

   1.

   2.

   3.

Chapter 3

CARPENTRY BELOW GROUND (SUBSTRUCTURE)

LEARNING OBJECTIVES

By the end of this chapter you will be able to:

- Demonstrate an understanding of the carpentry processes that take place below ground.

NOS REFERENCE

Conform to general workplace safety

Move and handle resources

SUBSTRUCTURE

Profile boards

> **Profile boards** Boards placed at the corners of a building to transfer the plan outline of a building onto the ground. They are held securely in place by square pegs and ranging lines are fixed to them to indicate the foundation, frontage line, right angle lines and back line.

> **Setting out** The process of marking out a plan on the ground of a site using profile boards connected by ranging lines.

The site carpenter may be asked to construct **profile boards**; these are wooden cross boards with square pegs attached. During the **setting out** process, the position of the foundations and walls are marked on the profile boards which are set well away from the planned excavations to allow sufficient working space, particularly if mechanical equipment is going to be used.

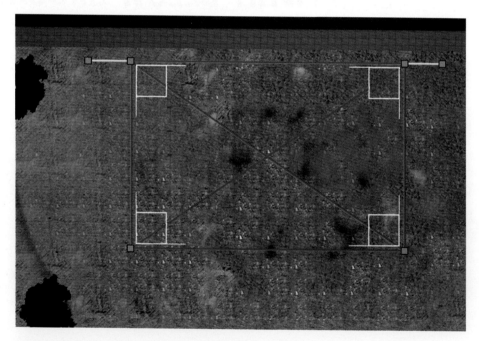

Profile boards used to set out building positions

Examples of profile boards

Trench support

Once the foundation trench has been excavated it will need support; the type and strength of this support will depend on the soil type around the excavation. Traditionally, the whole support system was made from timber. However excess pressure and extreme weather conditions can cause timber supports to fail so a combination of timber and steel supports is now often used.

Trench supports should include extended sides which provide a barrier against anything being kicked or knocked into the trench. This is known as a kicker and is similar to a toe board on a scaffold. Where this is not practical, the trench should be covered with the appropriate sheet material. A handrail should also be put in place for safety purposes.

The site carpenter may also need to construct timber ducts to be placed in the foundation trench while the concrete is poured. This provides a duct in the foundation through which service pipes and cables can be passed.

Kicker A wooden board used to stop anything being knocked into an empty trench.

Handrail A rail at the top of a balustrade which is usually fixed about waist height either horizontal or sloping.

A typical foundation trench

Foundation trench with metal support

ACTIVITY

What would cause a timber support to fail and what actions can be taken to prevent this happening?

Formwork

E-LEARNING

Use the e-learning programme to see an animated explanation of formwork.

The site carpenter may be asked to construct formwork which is designed to hold newly placed concrete, including paths and roads and large floor areas, until it has set. Formwork can be made of timber or steel but in either case must be straight and level, strong enough to hold the concrete without bending and have well-constructed joints so that the grout cannot escape. The choice between timber and steel formwork depends on the number of times the formwork is to be used.

Formwork should be left in place for a minimum of 12 hours, depending on the weather conditions after which it is 'struck' or removed from the concrete and cleaned thoroughly. Timber ducts can also be included in formwork if services are to be brought through the concrete.

Timber formwork

Metal formwork

ACTIVITY

What do you think are the advantages and disadvantages of timber and steel formwork?

Holding down bolt templates

E-LEARNING

Use the e-learning programme to see an animated explanation of holding down bolt templates.

In some buildings, a steel frame is used and steel members need to be attached to a concrete foundation. In this situation, a holding down bolt assembly that is cast into the concrete foundation is used. The carpenter may be asked to create a timber template to hold the bolts in position while the concrete is poured. The bolts are left protruding above the cast concrete so the steel member can be fixed to the foundation. When removing the formwork, care should be taken not to damage the bolts.

Steel frame inserted

Template and holding down bolts positioned

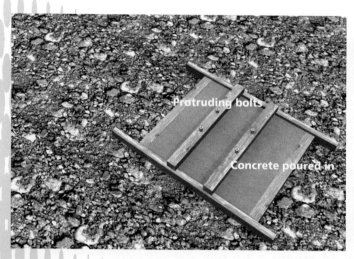

Concrete mix poured into the hole

Template removed with the bolts protruding

CHECK YOUR KNOWLEDGE

1. **What are the different parts of a timber trench support called? Label the image below.**

2. **List two features that are marked on a profile board.**

   1.

   2.

3. **List three uses for formwork.**

   1.

   2.

   3.

4. **What is the minimum amount of time that formwork should be left in place?**

☐ a. 6 hours

☐ b. 12 hours

☐ c. 24 hours

☐ d. 36 hours

☐ e. 48 hours

5. **Give an example of when a holding down bolt template may be used.**

Chapter 4

CARPENTRY ABOVE GROUND (SUPERSTRUCTURE/FIRST FIX)

LEARNING OBJECTIVES

By the end of this chapter you will:

- Understand the process of carcassing.

- Know about timber floor constructions.

- Understand joists and how they are constructed.

- Know about roof construction.

- Know about door and window frames.

CARCASSING

Carcassing in a building refers to the construction of the main structural elements of the building, including the ground floors, first floors, roofs, walls and partitions. All of these elements are usually constructed from sawn timber and covered with a decorative finish, e.g. floor boards or plaster boards. These elements are the 'bones' of the building; which is why the term carcass is used.

Stud partitions are part of carcassing

Ground floors

Suspended timber floor

E-LEARNING

Use the e-learning programme to see an animated explanation of suspended timber floors.

A suspended timber floor consists of a series of timber joists which span the floor covered with a timber decking. The joists generally span the shortest distance between walls and can be built into the inner leaf of the wall, suspended on joist hangers or supported by sleeper walls.

The distance between the joists will depend on the load expected to be supported by the floor, the span the joists will cover, the cross section size of the joists, the material the joists are made of and the decking material being used to cover the joists. Air must be allowed to circulate under these types of floors to prevent damp so air bricks should be fitted into the inner and outer leaf of the brickwork and the sleeper walls should be of honeycomb construction for the same reason. All timbers are placed on a damp proof course (DPC) to prevent damp rising from the sleeper walls to the timber.

Inner leaf The internal wall of a cavity construction which is commonly formed of blocks. If partial fill insulation cavity boards are used, they should be fixed to the inner leaf using special wall ties.

Sleeper wall A wall which is usually honeycombed in construction and is used to support the timber joists of a hollow ground floor.

Outer leaf The external wall of a cavity construction. The outer leaf wall is tied to the inner leaf using wall ties.

Air brick A perforated brick or metal unit of brick size which is built into a wall; used for ventilation.

ACTIVITY

From the information given, label this diagram of a suspended timber floor.

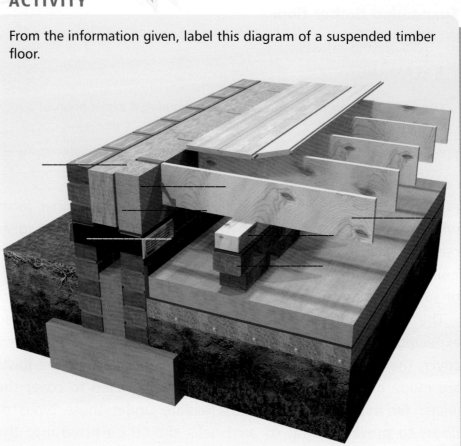

Solid ground floor with timber covering

Solid concrete floors are more durable than timber floors and are built into many modern domestic houses. These floors can be covered with a timber floor finish of various types including tongue and groove strips, chipboard, plywood or wooden blocks.

Whichever type of timber floor finish is chosen, it will need to be protected from any water vapour rising up from the subfloor and condensing in the space underneath the flooring. A vapour barrier, normally made of polythene, is generally used.

SUSTAINABILITY

Insulation can also be included underneath the timber floor finish to prevent heat loss.

ACTIVITY

From the information given, label this diagram of a solid ground floor with timber covering.

ACTIVITY

Use an internet search engine to research the latest Building Regulations regarding **U values** and insulation requirements.

Make a note of your findings and relevant web addresses below.

WEBLINKS

U value A measurement of the rate of heat loss through a wall, roof or floor which should be as low as possible to reduce the energy consumption of the building.

Floating timber floor

A floating timber floor is similar to a suspended timber floor in construction with a series of joists and a timber decking. The joists are laid directly onto a concrete subfloor and as they do not need to provide support they are smaller than those in a suspended floor. Insulation and **underfloor heating** can be laid between the joists for heating and also to make the floor quieter.

Underfloor heating
A type of heating provided by water pipes or electric elements in the screed or electric mats on the floor screed under a floor. Underfloor heating can be used under tiled floors.

ACTIVITY

From the information given, label this diagram of a floating timber floor.

Upper floors

Like ground floors, upper floors also consist of a series of joists supported at each end by the structural walls either by being built into the inner leaf of the brickwork or suspended on joist hangers. In a single floor, the joists span the width of the room but if an opening is required, for a staircase or chimney for example, other types of joists need to be included. These are known as trimming joists, trimmers and trimmed joists.

Standard sized joists are usually made from 50mm wide sawn timber but trimmers that support the bridging joists need to be thicker than this, usually 75mm wide.

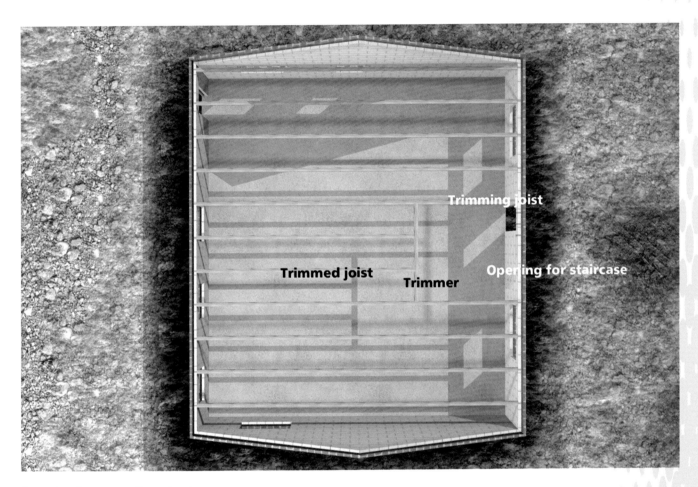

Example of an upper floor structure

The depth of the joist needed will depend on the span to be covered. You can find out more about joist spans by referring to the span tables in the Building Regulations. However, as a rough guide, you can calculate the depth required by dividing the span in millimetres by 20 and then adding 20. If the depth of the joist required becomes too great, additional supports will be required for the floor, the details of which are covered in the architectural drawings.

Here is an example of working out the depth of a joist required using the rough guide method discussed above.

Span is 3m	Span = 3000mm
Depth of the joist required is 3000 divided by 20 plus 20 which gives 170, therefore the joist would need to be 170mm deep.	(3000mm/20) + 20 = 170mm

ACTIVITY

Ask your tutor about the Building Regulations span tables. Using the rough guide method discussed, what would be the required depth of a joist for a span of 2.5m? Show your working out below.

Strutting and bridging

If the joist is to span more than 3.5m, extra support in the form of strutting or bridging will be needed.

Solid bridging

This method consists of timber struts that are the same depth as the joists. They are cut and fixed with nails at regular intervals between the joists. However, this technique allows the struts to become loose if the joists shrink.

Use of solid bridging

Herringbone strutting

Timber battens of around 50 × 25mm are fixed diagonally between the joists. This technique allows the struts to stay in place even if the joists shrink in size.

Use of herringbone strutting

Steel herringbone strutting

These are steel struts which are fixed diagonally between joists. However, they are usually made in preset sizes which may not always fit the space between the joists.

Use of steel herringbone strutting

Restraint straps

These are straps used where the joists run parallel to the inner leaf of the brickwork. They are fixed with nails and should be supported with noggings between the joists.

Use of restraint straps

ACTIVITY

Research each of these types of bridging and strutting. Where are they used and what are the advantages and disadvantages of each type?

WEBLINKS

Timber stud partitions

E-LEARNING

Use the e-learning programme to see an animated explanation of fitting timber stud partitions.

Timber stud partitions are a common way of dividing up an area into separate rooms. Studs and noggings are usually made from pieces of either 100mm × 50mm or 75mm × 50mm sawn timber depending on the requirements. Metal frameworks can also be used and consist of a similar structure.

Stud partitions can be pre-made and delivered to a site but this assumes that the floors and ceilings in the building are plumb and square. They have to be slightly smaller than the space they are meant to fit to enable them to be manoeuvred into place and they then need to be packed and wedged before being fixed into place.

Stud partition A lightweight, usually non-load-bearing timber frame wall.

Stud The timber posts within a timber frame wall or partition.

Noggings Short horizontal timber struts fitted between studs in a timber stud wall.

Plumb The vertical level of a surface or structure.

More commonly, stud partitions are constructed on-site. The timber is cut to size and the head is attached to the ceiling first, followed by the sole plate which must be plumb with the head plate. Next, the wall studs are added. Once this frame is complete the positions of the studs are marked; the distance between the studs will depend on the sheet material being used to cover the wall. Noggins are added last to provide stability. The joints in a stud partition are fixed with nailed butt joints, skew nailing or framing anchors.

Roof terminology

E-LEARNING

Use the e-learning programme to find out more information about each part of the roof.

ACTIVITY

The roof of a building can come in many different shapes and sizes and can be made up of numerous parts. From the labels, descriptions and image shown, work out what each part of the roof shown is called and what it's for.

Roof component	Description	Image label
Ridge	The triangular part at the top of a wall	
Verge	The roof line where two sloping roofs meet	
Hip	The lower part of the roof where it meets the wall	
Gable	The horizontal board fixed to the end of the rafters which usually includes ventilation	
Bargeboard	The top line of the roof where the two sloping surfaces meet	
Eaves	The line from ridge to eaves where two sloping roofs meet	
Valley	The eaves of a gable end that over-hang the roof	
Soffit	The fascia board around the verge of the roof that finishes a gable end	

Truss rafter roofs

The majority of modern domestic buildings use factory-made truss rafter roofs which have many advantages over traditional roofs constructed on-site. Truss rafter roofs can span a large area without the need for supporting walls underneath and are strong enough to support the roofing material above. They are available in a number of designs and their use allows a roof to be erected in a very short time compared with traditional cut roofs. This may play a large part in their selection and use; however, one of the main disadvantages of using a truss roof is the lack of loft space for storage in the completed roof.

An example of truss rafter roofs

ACTIVITY

What are each of these roof truss types called?

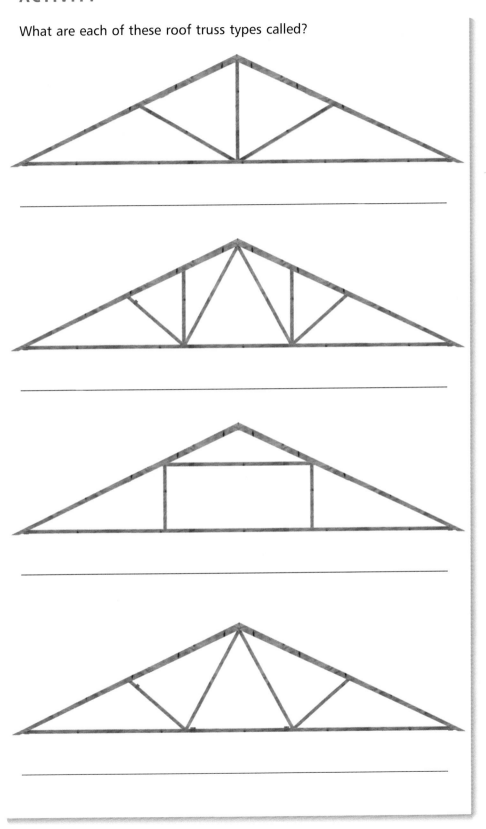

Fitting a truss rafter roof

Mortar A mixture of sand, cement (sometimes with lime and/or additives) and water, used to bond stones and bricks. Can be mixed by hand or mechanically on- or off-site.

E-LEARNING

Use the e-learning programme to see an animation of fitting a truss rafter roof.

To erect a truss rafter roof, first fix the wall plates to the top of the inner leaf. These should be laid on a **mortar** bed and fixed with holding down straps.

Fix the first truss to the wall plate using framing anchors or truss clips. There should be a gap of approximately 50mm between the end trusses and the **gable** end wall.

Gable The triangular upper part of a wall at the end of a ridged roof.

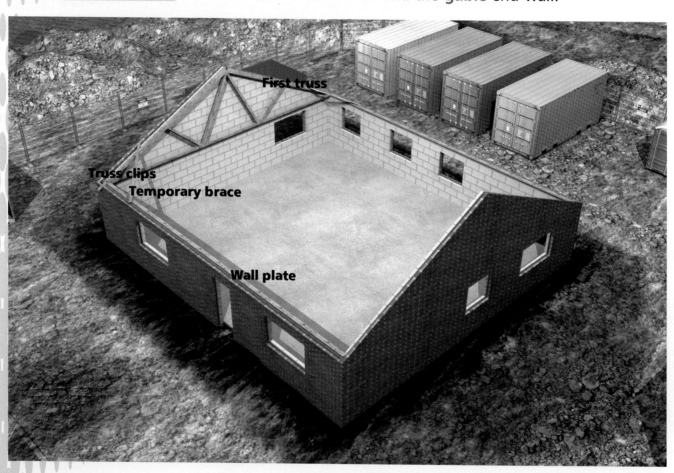

Fixing the first truss

Batten (carpentry) Horizontal lengths of timber fixed to the roof rafters to support the slates or tiles.

Hold the first truss in place with temporary braces. These should be attached diagonally from halfway along the truss to the wall plate on both sides and with a **batten** near the ridge of the truss towards the opposite gable end. Fix the remaining trusses to the wall plate and fix temporary battens between each truss at the base, middle and ridge of the truss on both sides.

Temporary batten

Temporary batten

Temporary batten

Temporary batten

Fixing remaining trusses and adding temporary battens

Attach a chevron or diagonal brace to the underside of the roof trusses. These should span from the corners of the building to the centre of the roof framework.

Attach longitudinal braces between each truss. These should be fixed on the underside of each diagonal and on top of the horizontal beams.

Horizontal restraint straps should then be fixed at a maximum of two metre intervals joining the end trusses to the inner leaf of the gable end. Finally, remove all temporary braces.

As roof trusses are designed and manufactured items, once on-site they should not be cut or altered in any way unless a design and instruction has been issued from the architect. If a roof has been altered without instruction it may fail and so invalidate the insurance and/or warranty from the manufacturer.

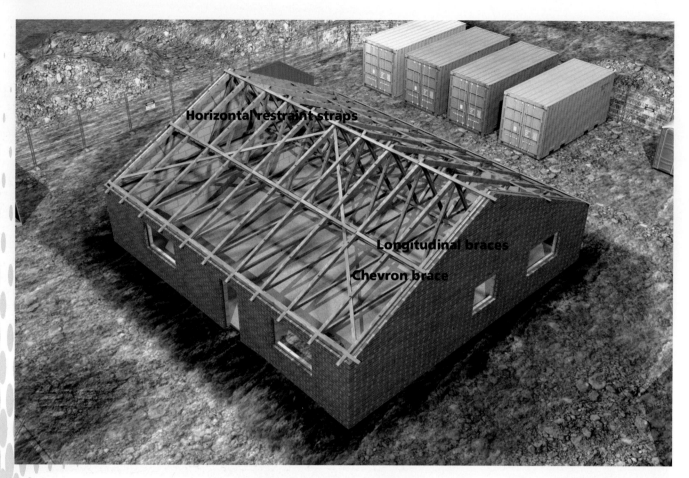

Adding braces and straps to secure roof in place

HEALTH & SAFETY

Pre-formed truss rafters are large and difficult to move. Care should be taken not to damage the trusses or cause injury to construction workers when they are being moved. If trusses are moved by hand it should be by a team of workers. Trusses should be kept upright when they are being moved and the correct manual handling procedures should be followed. If the trusses need to be moved to a great height a crane can be used together with slings and a guide rope to move the trusses into place.

PREPARED TIMBER

Door frames and linings

The main differences between a frame and a lining are that a frame is usually placed in the external walls of a building and is commonly constructed of larger sized and more durable timber to withstand weather damage. It is also stronger and therefore provides a more secure fixing for the external doors and increased security. Linings are usually placed internally, so do not have the same need to withstand weather. Some linings may be made of larger size timbers if they are to provide a secure opening within the building.

Door frames sit in the openings in walls where doors are to be hung. They consist of a number of components which are held together with mortice and tenon joints.

ACTIVITY

Do you know what the different components of a door frame are called? Match the labels with the correct part of the diagram.

Label	Diagram number
Jambs	
Cill / Threshold	
Head	
Transom	

Cill The board at the external base of a window; designed to ensure water runs away from the building.

A door frame with a **cill** is called a closed door frame and a door frame without a cill is an open door frame. Open frames are used where ease of access is important, for example in shops, public buildings and for wheelchair access. If a transom is included, the top part of the frame may be glazed with a sky-light type window and these frames may be termed 'storey frames' if they reach the ceiling. Door frames can be made from softwood or hardwood but if a softwood frame is used, the cill must be hardwood for durability.

A closed door frame

An open door frame

Door frames can be fixed into a building as the brickwork progresses using specially designed ties which are cemented into joints in the brickwork. Alternatively they can be fixed into preformed openings once the brickwork is complete. If the frames are to be added when the brickwork is complete, temporary frames called profiles are used to create the correct sized opening in the brickwork. Once the brickwork is complete, the door frames are fixed to the brickwork with screws and rawlplugs.

Rawlplug A fastener (usually plastic) which helps screws to be fitted tightly into a masonry wall.

Door frame as brickwork progresses

The frame fixed into the brickwork

Door profile to preserve the opening

> **Reveal** The sides of door and window openings which should be identified when setting out the first and second course of bricks. This is to ensure that there are no unbroken perpends throughout the height of the wall.

Door linings are generally used on internal doors and unlike door frames, cover the entire door **reveal**. They are held in place with temporary battens until the work is complete. Door linings are usually fixed in place before the plaster is applied to internal walls and are used to help guide the thickness of the plaster finish.

Using the site datum, all heads should be set at the same height throughout the building. The legs will rest directly onto wooden floors but a small gap should be left at the bottom of legs above a concrete floor to allow the final layer of screed to be applied. Door linings can be fixed in place using a variety of fixings but screws are the common type of fixing used.

An internal door lining

Windows

Windows are designed to allow light and air into a room and to keep the heat in and the weather out. Traditional casement windows are made of softwood or hardwood but can also be made from metal or **uPVC**. Wooden casement windows are usually added to a building as the brickwork progresses and are held with frame clamps that have been bedded into the mortar between bricks. Other window types are built into pre-formed openings once brickwork is complete. In this case, temporary frames called profiles are used to create the correct sized opening in the brickwork. Once the brickwork is complete, window frames are fixed into place with screws and rawlplugs.

Within a window frame, a window that is fixed and doesn't open is called direct glazing, whereas a window that opens is called a sash or casement. The direction that the sash or casement will open will be indicated by diagonal lines on the drawings for the building.

> **uPVC** A type of stable plastic used in the manufacture of double glazed window frames, doors and cladding.

Wooden casement windows

Window profile to preserve the opening

ACTIVITY

A window is made up of a number of parts. Find the following terms in the wordsearch.

X	S	V	A	O	P	F	M	G	A	F	I	F
Q	M	O	S	N	A	R	T	N	N	A	T	O
M	H	Z	T	X	P	L	B	I	T	S	N	T
B	V	M	H	P	H	V	A	Z	M	B	E	R
M	E	N	C	J	C	N	F	A	R	I	M	H
A	D	E	L	J	I	O	I	L	L	T	E	F
R	A	A	A	E	L	I	C	G	Q	P	S	J
V	S	M	E	S	L	L	S	T	M	L	A	V
N	B	R	C	H	H	L	N	C	F	V	C	K
G	Q	B	P	E	S	U	U	E	Y	W	U	J
A	A	M	T	U	A	M	M	R	D	V	D	Z
Q	C	Q	D	S	S	G	Q	I	V	A	Y	H
T	V	T	I	G	C	Z	C	D	F	P	Y	Q

CILL, HEAD, JAMB, MULLION, TRANSOM, DIRECT GLAZING, SASH, CASEMENT

ACTIVITY

Do you know where the different components of a window are? Match the labels with the correct part of the diagram.

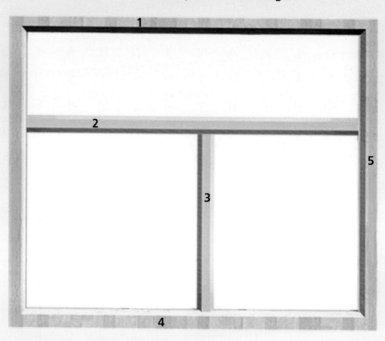

Label	Diagram number
Cill	
Head	
Jamb	
Mullion	
Transom	

Staircases

NOTE ON UK STANDARDS

Care must be taken when constructing a staircase as the design and construction are covered by Building Regulations. The width of the stairs, the minimum **balustrade** height and the size of the risers and treads are all strictly controlled depending on where the staircase is being built and what it will be used for.

Balustrade A collective term for the balusters and handrail on a set of stairs.

Staircases are large expensive products consisting of many components which are usually delivered to site as complete as possible. The carpenter will then need to construct the remaining components, for example the **newel posts**, balustrade and handrail leaving a consistent head room of at least 2m. The staircase is fixed either to an outside wall or suspended on a trimmer joist.

As constructing the staircase is a first fix trade, it will need to be protected from damage whilst the project is completed. Hardboard should be pinned temporarily to the top of each tread and sometimes also to the newel post for protection.

> **Newel post** Vertical post which supports the handrail on a set of stairs.

ACTIVITY

A staircase is made up of a number of parts. Find the following staircase terms in the wordsearch.

B	U	L	L	N	O	S	E	S	T	E	P
R	E	S	I	R	C	G	A	P	E	F	D
F	N	T	V	X	G	L	G	Y	D	G	K
S	S	R	X	I	N	I	E	F	A	T	Z
R	A	E	Y	V	I	A	G	Y	R	S	H
E	F	A	K	Y	R	R	J	I	T	O	Q
T	X	D	F	I	T	D	L	D	S	P	S
S	Z	H	M	C	S	N	L	X	U	L	C
U	Y	E	N	L	L	A	G	S	L	E	S
L	T	D	J	C	L	H	K	A	L	W	Y
A	U	H	K	F	A	R	L	V	A	E	I
B	N	E	X	Q	W	V	Q	A	B	N	A

TREAD, RISER, BALUSTRADE, NEWEL POST, HANDRAIL, BALUSTERS, BULLNOSE STEP, WALL STRING

ACTIVITY

Do you know where the different components of a staircase are? Match the labels with the correct part of the diagram.

Label	Diagram number
Tread	
Riser	
Balustrade	
Newel post	
Handrail	
Baluster	
Wall string	

CHECK YOUR KNOWLEDGE

1. **When is strutting or bridging used with floor joists?**

   ☐ a. When the span is greater than 2.5m

   ☐ b. When the span is greater than 3m

   ☐ c. When the span is greater than 4.5m

2. **If a window or door is to be added once the brickwork is complete, what is the name of the structure that creates the correct sized space in the brickwork as it is built?**

   ☐ a. Prefile

   ☐ b. Profile

   ☐ c. Proforma

3. **What is the construction of the main structural timber in a building called?**

4. **List one advantage and one disadvantage of factory constructed truss rafter roofs.**

   Advantage:

   Disadvantage:

5. **What is the difference between direct glazing and a casement window?**

Chapter 5

FINISHES (SECOND FIX)

LEARNING OBJECTIVES

By the end of this chapter you will:

- Know about doors, ironmongery and mouldings.

- Know about service encasements and fitments.

DOORS, IRONMONGERY AND MOULDINGS

Doors

Interior and exterior doors come in a number of styles depending on where they are to be hung and their purpose.

Generally speaking, interior doors provide privacy, a thermal and sound barrier and sometimes fire resistance. They are usually lightweight, cheap and can be hung on a door lining using only two hinges.

External doors provide the same features as internal doors together with security and weather resistance. They are generally heavier and more expensive than interior doors. An exterior door has to be hung using three hinges and will sometimes include a **door threshold** or cill and **draft proofing** as it is exposed to the elements.

Door threshold The board at the base of an external door; designed to ensure water runs away from the building.

Draft proofing A cheap and efficient way of saving energy in a building by blocking openings which may let in cold air and let out warm air.

An interior door

An exterior door

Hanging doors

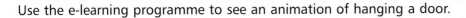

E-LEARNING

Use the e-learning programme to see an animation of hanging a door.

The methods of hanging interior and exterior doors are very similar apart from the number of hinges. First, the door should be shaped to fit the door lining or frame leaving a 2–3mm gap and without binding when it closes. While the door is temporarily held in the frame or lining the position of the hinges is marked. You should measure 150mm down from the top of the door for the top hinge and 225mm up from the bottom of the door for the bottom hinge. When hanging an external door the middle hinge is marked halfway between these positions.

When the door is removed from the frame the recesses of the hinges on the door and frame can be more accurately marked with a gauge or square and then cut out with a chisel. The hinges are then attached to the door using all the screws required. Once the hinges are attached to the door, it is placed again into the door frame and the hinges are attached to the frame with one screw in each hinge. This allows the carpenter to check that the door opens and closes without binding. Once this has been checked the remaining screws can be added to the hinges.

Mark the position of the hinges on the door

Cut out marked area with a chisel

Attach hinges to the door

Hang door to door frame and position correctly

Secure door to frame with remaining screws

ACTIVITY

List four tools that you would need to hang a door.

1.

2.

3.

4.

Ironmongery

E-LEARNING

Use the e-learning programme to see an animation of adding a mortice lock.

Ironmongery is sometimes also referred to as door furniture and as well as hinges includes locks, latches, letter plates and handles which are fixed to the door or door frame.

To add a mortice lock to a door, mark out the position of the lock on the **door stile** or edge of the door. Use a drill to create a series of holes to the correct depth and then finish off with a chisel to leave the correct sized and shaped opening for the lock.

Door stile The vertical member of a panelled door, where the hinges and locks are fixed in place.

Mark lock position on door stile

Create an opening in the door

To mark around the faceplate, place the lock in the recess and mark with a sharp knife then remove sufficient wood with a chisel so that the faceplate will sit flush with the stile. Mark the positions of the spindle for the handle and the lock and use a drill to create the holes needed. Finally, fix the lock and handles in place with all the screws required.

Ensure faceplate is flush with door

Create holes for handle and lock

Fix lock and handle in place

The striking plate should be fixed to the correct position in the frame using the same methods before checking that the lock works properly.

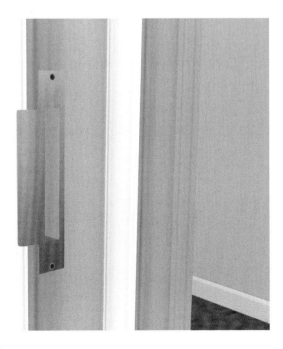

Fix striking plate in the door frame

ACTIVITY

List four tools that you would need to fit a mortice lock.

1.

2.

3.

4.

Skirting A decorative board at the junction between the walls and floor of a room.

Picture rail A moulding positioned along a wall a short distance down from the ceiling.

Dado rail A moulding attached along a wall separating the upper and lower areas of a wall.

Mouldings

Mouldings provide a decorative finish as well as protection on some surfaces. The two main types of mouldings used in buildings are architraves and **skirting** boards. Architraves are used to hide the joint between door frames and the wall and provide a decorative finish. Skirting boards cover the joint between the floor and the wall and give a strong finish to the base of the wall. Other types of mouldings include cornices, **picture rails**, **dado rails** and plinth blocks.

ACTIVITY

Match the types of mouldings with their correct position on the diagram.

Label	Diagram number
Picture rail	
Cornice	
Skirting board	
Dado rail	
Architrave	
Plinth block	

Fitting mouldings

E-LEARNING

Use the e-learning programme to see an animation of fitting mouldings.

As mouldings need to fit the corners around door frames and the internal and external corners of walls, they need to be cut to fit these shapes. Scribe joints are used on internal corners where one piece of moulding is cut or shaped so it butts up against another. Mouldings may need to be scribed to fit uneven **backgrounds**, for example skirting boards on uneven floors. In this case the moulding is fitted temporarily, marked against the background and then scribed to fit using a saw, plane or sander depending on how much timber needs to be removed.

Backgrounds General term used for the surface to which materials are adhered.

Internal corner with scribed joint

Architrave Can be a horizontal lintel from one column to another or the border/ moulding around a door frame.

Mitre joints are used on **architraves** around doors and also on mouldings to fit external corners of walls. When fixing mouldings to a wall you should work in one direction around the room so that the joints are not visible from the doorway. Mouldings are fixed to the wall using nails or screws through the face of the moulding; the type will depend on the background it is being fixed to. Mouldings which are to be painted can have screw and nail heads filled with filler but mouldings which are to be polished will need to be pelleted.

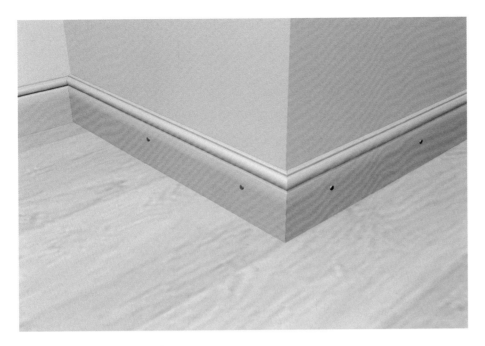

External corner with mitred joint

SERVICE ENCASEMENTS AND FITMENTS

Service encasements

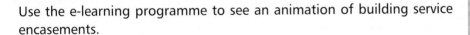

E-LEARNING

Use the e-learning programme to see an animation of building service encasements.

Service encasements are the frames and sheet material cladding that are used to cover things like pipe work, cables, steel beams and unused spaces, e.g. under baths. The sheet material will vary depending on where it is being used but the basic principle is the same.

First, the correct sized frame is constructed in much the same way as timber studwork. The frames are then attached to wooden battens fixed to the wall. Sheet material cladding is then fixed to the frame. Where pipes will protrude from the encasement, a face panel is scribed and cut before being fixed around the pipe. Where pipes run along the bottom of a wall, skirting boards can be used as part of the cladding for the frame. They may also need to include a removable panel for access to a stop cock.

Casement fixed to wooden battens

Cut-out panel for protruding pipes

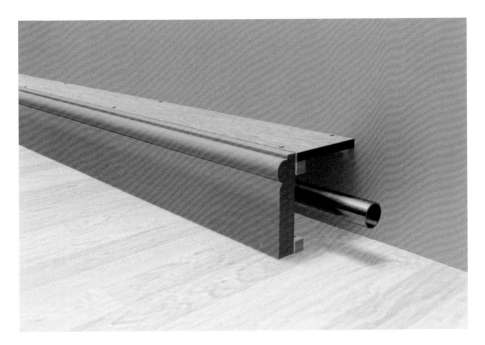

Fascias can be added to the casements

ACTIVITY

Why do you need to be careful when drilling into walls and floors? Give two reasons below.

1.

2.

Fitting base units

Kitchen units can be supplied ready formed or as flat packs and come in a range of sizes. To fit base units, use the site datum to draw a datum line approximately 1m above the floor around the walls that will have units fitted. A level back rail is fixed to the wall below the datum line at a user friendly height for the units, remembering to allow for the thickness of the worktop.

Working from the highest point, the units can now be placed in line with the back rail and adjusted to level using the legs of the units. Carefully measured spaces are left for appliances until all the units are in place which can then be fixed to the wall or floors using connecting bolts or screws.

Draw a datum line, approx. 1m from the floor

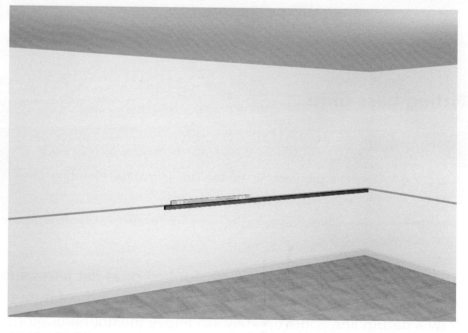

Attach a level batten to the line

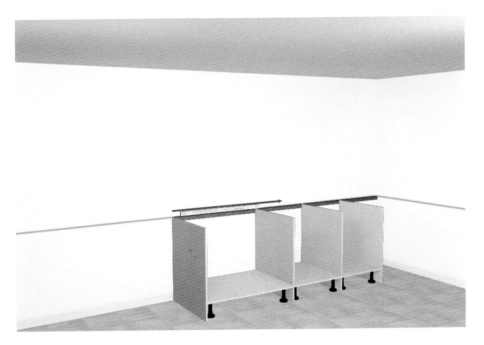

Fix the units to the batten, starting at the highest point

Adjust the height of the unit legs where necessary

Leave enough room for any appliances

Fitting worktops

E-LEARNING

Use the e-learning programme to see an animation of fitting worktops.

Worktops first need to be cut to the correct length. If an internal corner is needed the worktop is cut at 45° through the curved edge and then straight through the remaining piece of worktop. This is sometimes known as a mason's mitre. The join is held using biscuit joints or a metal clamp secured under the worktop holding the two pieces together.

Housing for appliances is marked and then cut on the face of the worktop with a special downward cutting jigsaw blade to avoid damage to the surface of the worktop. Worktops are very hard to mark with a pencil or marker so the use of some masking tape to allow easier marking of the shape to be cut and also to help protect the surface is advisable. Finally, the worktops are attached to the top of the base units using screws and L-shaped connectors.

Mark out area to be cut

Fix appliance in cut area

Units joined together with appropriate fixings

ACTIVITY

How would you cut this worktop so it fits in the corner of this kitchen? Mark on the diagram where you would cut it.

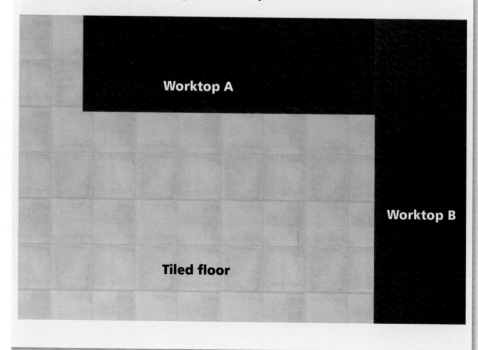

Fitting wall units

Wall units need to be hung with sufficient space between the worktop and the unit but the actual measurement can vary. Once the height has been established, work up from the datum line and mark a point that shows the space required plus the height of the unit.

Wall units are then either fixed directly to the wall or hung on adjustable brackets which vary in design from manufacturer to manufacturer. Hook the wall units into the steel hanger plates working in one direction around the room. If you are using adjustable brackets, you can adjust them using the screw in the bracket and, once the units are all level, the bracket can be tightened onto the steel hanger plate.

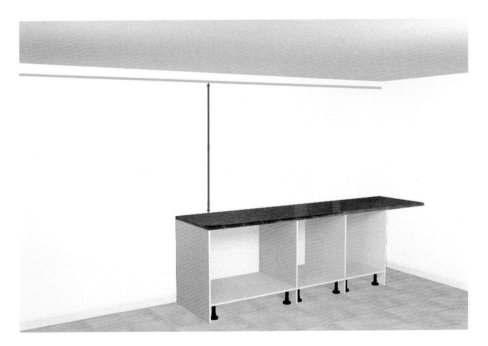

Measure where the wall units need to be positioned

Attach the hanger plates

Fix wall units to the hanger plates

ACTIVITY

Approximately how far above the datum line would you mark the line to hang the wall units if the space required above the floor units is 450mm and the wall units are 726mm high?

Show your working out below.

Finishing off

Finishing off includes adding plinth boards, **cornices**, pelmets, shelves, doors and drawers. Plinth boards cover the space between the bottom of the base unit and the floor. They are attached using clips so they can be removed fairly easily if necessary and may need to be cut to fit uneven floors. Cornices finish off the top of wall units and pelmets can be added to the bottom to hide any integral lighting that may be included. Doors and shelves are added to units last to avoid damage.

Cornice A decorative moulding at the junction between the walls and ceiling of a room.

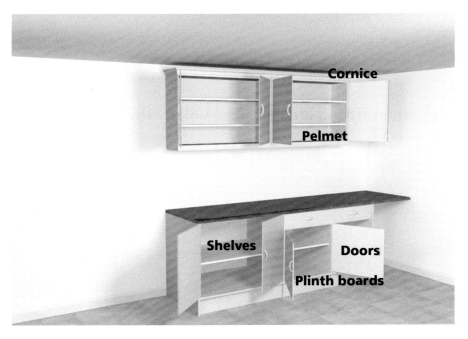

Finishing off the units

CHECK YOUR KNOWLEDGE

1. **What size should the gap between a finished door and the door frame be?**

   ☐ a. 1–2mm

   ☐ b. 2–3mm

   ☐ c. 3–4mm

2. **List three features of internal doors.**

   1.

   2.

   3.

3. **How far down from the top of the door should you measure to attach the top hinge?**

   ☐ a. 50mm

   ☐ b. 100mm

   ☐ c. 150mm

4. **List three reasons why a carpenter may be required to construct a service encasement.**

   1.

   2.

   3.

5. **When fitting kitchen base units, where should you start?**

   ☐ a. The highest point

   ☐ b. The lowest point

   ☐ c. At the door frame

Chapter 6

END TEST

END TEST OBJECTIVES

The end test will check your knowledge on the information held within this book.

The Test

E-LEARNING

Use the e-learning programme to complete this test online.

1. At what stages of a project is the site carpenter involved?

☐ a. Planning

☐ b. Setting out

☐ c. Substructure (below ground)

☐ d. Superstructure (first fix)

☐ e. Finishing (second fix)

☐ f. Sales

2. What is the symbol for an Ordnance Survey bench mark?

☐ a.

☐ b.

☐ c.

3. Decay can occur when the moisture in timber goes above what percentage?

4. Which of these is a mitre joint and which is a scribe joint?

☐ a.

☐ b.

5. List four things that you should check before using any power tool.

1.

2.

3.

4.

6. What are the three sustainable methods of dealing with waste materials?

7. You need 5m of softwood timber that is available in 1.8m lengths. How many lengths do you need to order?

8. Timber that is of insufficient quality cannot be recycled. True or false?

☐ a. True

☐ b. False

9. What is the purpose of formwork?

☐ a. To mark the position of the foundation trenches

☐ b. To support the sides of foundation trenches

☐ c. To hold newly placed concrete until it is set

10. If the span of an upper floor is 3.5m, how deep in millimetres do the joists need to be?

11. A disadvantage of solid bridging between floor joists is that it can become loose as the joists shrink. True or false?

☐ a. True

☐ b. False

12. What are these areas of a roof called? Label the areas of the roof.

13. What are the steps taken to construct a truss rafter roof? Number the activities below in the correct order.

☐ Attach a chevron brace each side

☐ Attach longitudinal braces

☐ Attach temporary braces each side of ridge

☐ Space out and fix all other trusses

☐ Fix horizontal restraint straps on trusses at gable ends

☐ Fix first truss to wall plate

☐ Fix second truss and attach to wall plate and battens

☐ Fix wall plates to top of inner leaf

☐ Hold first truss with temporary brace

14. What are the different parts of a door frame called? Label the different parts of a door frame on the figure below.

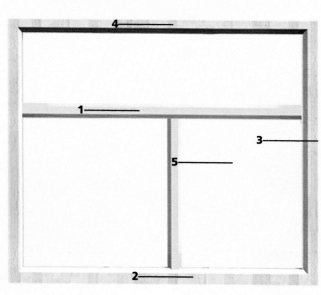

15. What are the different parts of a window frame called? Label the different parts of a window frame on the figure below.

16. What are the different parts of a staircase called? Label the different parts of a staircase on the figure below.

17. Why do you use only one screw per hinge when initially attaching a door to a frame?

☐ a. To check the screws are the right length

☐ b. To check the door doesn't catch

☐ c. In case the door is in the wrong frame

18. What are these different types of mouldings called? Label the different types of moulding on the figure below.

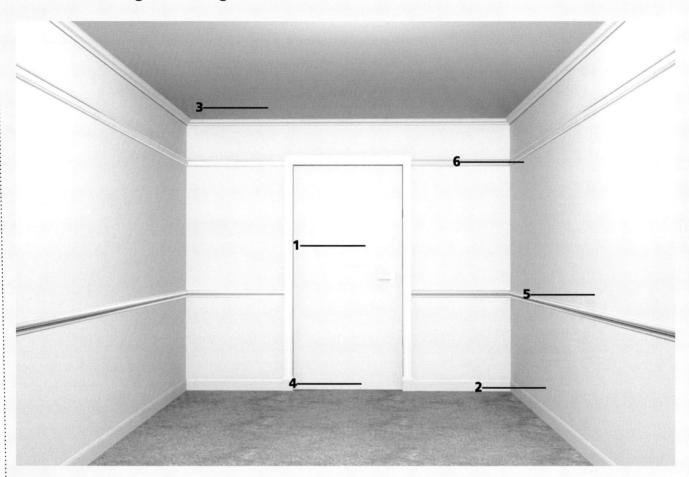

19. Wall units are hung on a wooden batten fixed to the wall. True or false?

☐ a. True

☐ b. False

20. Where are cornices, pelmets and plinth boards placed to finish off wall and base units? Label the diagram below.

Answers to Check Your Knowledge and End Test

CHAPTER 1

1. **B & C: The height of an Ordnance Survey Bench Mark can be obtained from the local authority planning office or an ordnance survey map.**

2. **A, B, F & G: These are all forms of written communication. In addition, minutes of a meeting or meeting notes would enable you to keep a written record of verbal communication at a meeting.**

3. **Scale is 1:100. 100mm will represent 10,000mm or 10m.**

4. **A bill of quantities will contain a list of *materials* that need to be used and their *quantities*.**

5. **The temporary datum peg must be positioned where it will not be disturbed by any construction activity and should be protected by a small wooden fence.**

CHAPTER 2

1. **F: The dust created when machining MDF is carcinogenic and therefore the use of it is listed as a health risk.**

2. **51: $150m^2/2.97m^2 = 50.505$ rounded up to 51.**

3. **True: Sheet materials can be stored vertically as well as horizontally as long as they are stored upright in specially made racks that are the correct size to prevent bowing of the materials while still allowing easy access and removal.**

4. **Where the wood is of insufficient quality it can be recycled as mulch, a composting agent, pet bedding, equestrian surfacing, chipboard or MDF.**

CHAPTER 3

1.

1 - Hand rail

2 - Kicker

3 - Poling boards

5 - Puncheons

4 - Wallings

6 - Struts

7 - Sole plate

2. During the setting out process, the position of the foundations and walls are marked on the profile boards.

3. Formwork is designed to hold newly placed concrete, including paths, roads and large floor areas, until it has set.

4. B: Formwork should be left in place for a minimum of 12 hours.

5. In some buildings, a steel frame is used and steel members need to be attached to a concrete foundation. In this situation, a holding down bolt assembly that is cast into the concrete foundation is used.

CHAPTER 4

1. B: If the joist is to span more than 3m, extra support in the form of strutting or bridging will be needed.

2. B: When windows are built into pre-formed openings once brickwork is complete, temporary frames called profiles are used to create the correct sized opening in the brickwork.

3. Carcassing refers to the construction of the main structural timber elements of a building, including the ground floors, first floors, roofs, walls and partitions.

4. The advantages are truss rafter roofs can span a large area without the need for supporting walls underneath and are strong enough to support the roofing material above. A disadvantage is the lack of loft space for storage in the completed roof.

5. Direct glazing does not open whereas a casement window does.

CHAPTER 5

1. B: The door should be shaped to fit in the door lining or frame leaving a 2–3mm gap and without binding when it closes.

2. Internal doors provide privacy, a thermal and sound barrier and fire resistance. They are lightweight, cheap and can be hung on a door lining using only two hinges.

3. C: While the door is temporarily held in the frame or lining, the position of the hinges is marked. You should measure about 150mm down from the top of the door for the top hinge.

4. Service encasements can cover pipe work, cables, steel beams and unused spaces, e.g. under baths.

5. A: When fitting kitchen base units, you should start at the highest point and adjust the rest of the units to this level.

CHAPTER 6

Please check your answers against the following. If any of the questions you answered are incorrect you are advised to go back to that section in the workbook or the e-learning programme to re-study.

Question 1

B, C, D, E: The carpenter is involved in the setting out, substructure, superstructure and finishing stages of a project.

Question 2

Question 3

Decay can occur in timber when the moisture in the wood goes above 20%.

Scribed joint

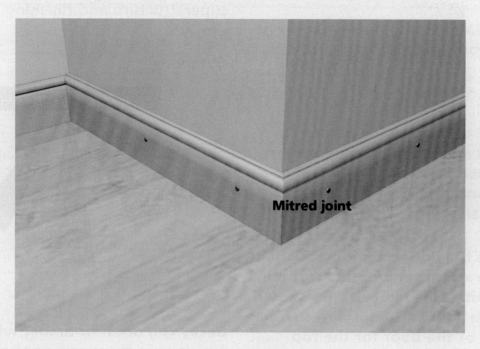

Mitred joint

Question 5

Correct answers can be from the following:

1. Are you familiar with the tool?
2. Do you have the correct PPE?
3. Do you know the correct procedure in the event of an accident?
4. Have you had the appropriate training?
5. Is the tool connected to a safe power supply?
6. Is the tool working correctly?

Question 6

The three sustainable methods of dealing with waste materials are: Reduce, Resuse and Recycle.

Question 7

5m/1.8m = 2.77 which is rounded up to 3.

Question 8

False: Timber can be recycled in a number of ways.

Question 9

C: The purpose of making formwork is to hold newly placed concrete until it has set.

Question 10

3500/20+20 = 195mm.

Question 11

True: Solid bridging between floor joists can become loose as joists shrinks.

Question 12

2 - Ridge

1 - Verge

5 - Hip

8 - Valley

4 - Gable

6 - Eaves

7 - Soffit

3 - Bargeboard

Question 13

1. Fix wall plates to top of inner leaf.
2. Fix first truss to wall plate.
3. Hold first truss with temporary brace.
4. Attach temporary braces each side of ridge.
5. Fix second truss and attach to wall plate and battens.
6. Space out and fix all other trusses.
7. Attach a chevron brace each side.
8. Attach longitudinal braces.
9. Fix horizontal restraint straps on trusses at gable ends.

Question 14

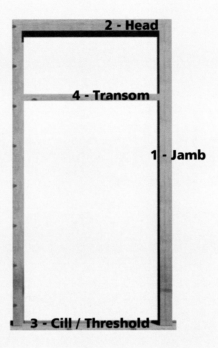

2 - Head

4 - Transom

1 - Jamb

3 - Cill / Threshold

Question 15

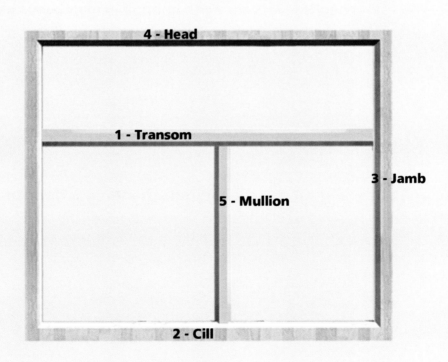

4 - Head

1 - Transom

3 - Jamb

5 - Mullion

2 - Cill

Question 16

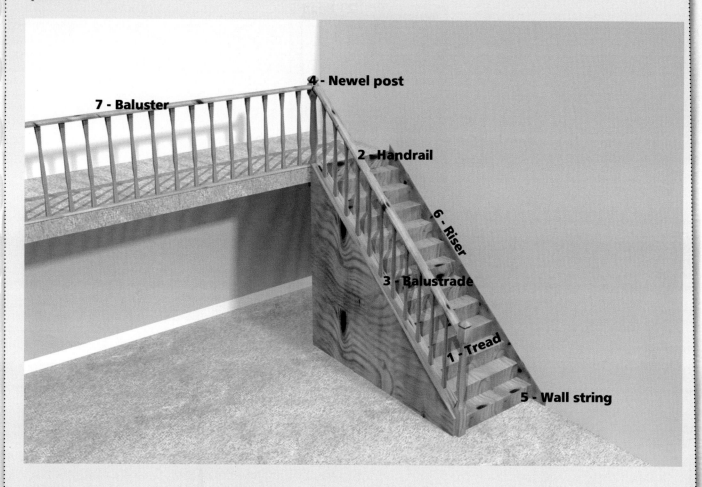

7 - Baluster
4 - Newel post
2 - Handrail
6 - Riser
3 - Balustrade
1 - Tread
5 - Wall string

Question 17

B: You only use one screw per hinge when initially hanging a door to make sure the door doesn't catch.

Question 18

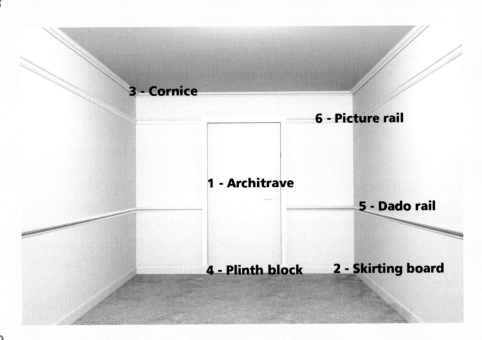

Question 19

False: Wall units are usually hung on steel battens.

Question 20

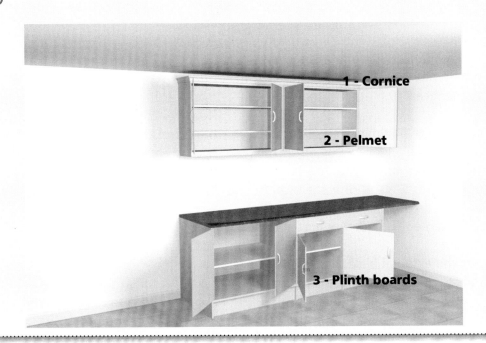

Glossary

Adhesive General term for a range of bonding agents.

Air brick A perforated brick or metal unit of brick size which is built into a wall; used for ventilation.

Air (natural) seasoning The means of drying timber by exposing it to the air and storing in a clean and dry place.

Architrave Can be a horizontal lintel from one column to another or the border/moulding around a door frame.

Arris (carpentry) The external edge of two surfaces, especially wood and panel doors.

Backgrounds General term used for the surface to which materials are adhered.

Balustrade A collective term for the balusters and handrail on a set of stairs.

Batten (carpentry) Horizontal lengths of timber fixed to the roof rafters to support the slates or tiles.

British Standards A set of standards to ensure the quality of goods and services.

Carcinogenic Chemicals or materials which can increase the risk of cancer. Personal protective equipment should always be worn whenever working with chemicals or materials that are carcinogenic.

Cement A grey or white powdery material made from chalk or limestone and clay. Cement is the most common binder in bricklaying mortar and works by hardening as a result of a chemical reaction when mixed with water. The most common type of cement is Ordinary Portland Cement (OPC).

Cill The board at the external base of a window; designed to ensure water runs away from the building.

Coniferous tree A type of evergreen tree which produces its fruit in the form of cones.

Cornice A decorative moulding at the junction between the walls and ceiling of a room.

Dado rail A moulding attached along a wall separating the upper and lower areas of a wall.

Datum peg Square timber peg used to mark the height of the brickwork up to damp proof course (DPC) level.

Deciduous trees Trees which lose all of their leaves for part of the year.

Door threshold The board at the base of an external door; designed to ensure water runs away from the building.

Door stile The vertical member of a panelled door, where the hinges and locks are fixed in place.

Draft proofing A cheap and efficient way of saving energy in a building by blocking openings which may let in cold air and let out warm air.

Drill bit A cutting tool which fits securely into the drill to create a cylindrical hole.

FSC Forest Stewardship Council.

Fundamental Bench Marks (FBMs) These bench marks are the realization of Ordnance Datum Newlyn across the country, from which many thousands of lower order bench marks have been created.

Fungicide A chemical used to kill or slow down fungal decay on timber.

Gable The triangular upper part of a wall at the end of a ridged roof.

Handrail A rail at the top of a balustrade which is usually fixed about waist height either horizontal or sloping.

Inner leaf The internal wall of a cavity construction which is commonly formed of blocks. If partial fill insulation cavity boards are used, they should be fixed to the inner leaf using special wall ties.

Ironmongery Products that have been manufactured from metal.

Joist A beam that supports a ceiling or floor.

Joist hangers Metal slots installed to wall plates, rafters or existing joists to support a row of joists. Available in different sizes to accommodate different joists.

Kicker A wooden board used to stop anything being knocked into an empty trench.

Kiln seasoning The means of drying timber by exposing it to heat using a number of techniques.

Level The horizontal level of a surface or structure.

Lintel A horizontal beam of timber (old buildings), stone, concrete or steel (new buildings) spanning the openings, e.g. doors and windows in a wall to support the structure above.

Mitre Two 45° joints formed to make a right angle joint.

Mortar A mixture of sand, cement (sometimes with lime and/or additives) and water, used to bond stones and bricks. Can be mixed by hand or mechanically on- or off-site.

Newel post Vertical posts which support the handrail on a set of stairs.

Noggings Short horizontal timber struts fitted between studs in a timber stud wall.

Ordnance Datum Newlyn The national height system for Great Britain which takes its base height from Newlyn in Cornwall.

Ordnance Survey Bench Marks (OSBMs) Measure height of the land above or below mean sea level.

Outer leaf The external wall of a cavity construction. The outer leaf wall is tied to the inner leaf using wall ties.

Packaging directive A government enforced directive which aims to control the amount of packaging which can be disposed of in landfill.

Personal Protective Equipment (PPE) Depending on the type of work, there are different types of equipment specifically designed to protect your health and safety. Examples include gloves, safety boots, goggles and dust mask.

Picture rail A moulding positioned along a wall a short distance down from the ceiling.

Plumb The vertical level of a surface or structure.

PPE The standard and widely used abbreviation for Personal Protective Equipment (see definition above).

Profile boards Boards placed at the corners of a building to transfer the plan outline of a building onto the ground. They are held securely in place by square pegs and ranging lines are fixed to it to indicate the foundation, frontage line, right angle lines and back line.

Rawlplug A fastener (usually plastic) which helps screws to be fitted tightly into a masonry wall.

Reveal The sides of door and window openings which should be identified when setting out the first and second course of bricks. This is to ensure that there are no unbroken perpends throughout the height of the wall.

Roof truss The timber frame structure of a roof, usually factory made and delivered to site.

Setting out The process of marking out a plan on the ground of a site using profile boards connected by ranging lines.

Skirting A decorative board at the junction between the walls and floor of a room.

Sleeper wall A wall which is usually honeycombed in construction and is used to support the timber joists of a hollow ground floor.

Spirit level A tool used to check true vertical and horizontal lines indicated by a bubble in spirit-filled vials.

Stud The timber posts within a timber frame wall or partition.

Stud partition A lightweight, usually non-load-bearing timber frame wall.

Sustainable materials Materials that have been sourced by causing little or no damage to the environment.

U value A measurement of the rate of heat loss through a wall, roof or floor which should be as low as possible to reduce the energy consumption of the building.

Underfloor heating A type of heating provided by water pipes or electric elements in the screed or electric mats on the floor screed under a floor. Underfloor heating can be used under tiled floors.

uPVC A type of stable plastic used in the manufacture of double glazed window frames, doors and cladding.

Veneer Very thin sheets of finely grained woods used to improve the aesthetics and strength of sheet materials, e.g. blockboard.

Wall plate A horizontal timber bedded in mortar on top of the wall. This provides the levelling and fixing point for ceiling joists, rafters and roof truss.

Index